THE ECOLOGY OF DEMOCRACY

FINDING WAYS TO HAVE A STRONGER HAND IN SHAPING OUR FUTURE

DAVID MATHEWS

Kettering Foundation Press

The Ecology of Democracy: Finding Ways to Have a Stronger Hand in Shaping Our Future is published by the Kettering Foundation Press. The interpretations and conclusions contained in the book represent the views of the author. They do not necessarily reflect the views of the Charles F. Kettering Foundation, its directors, or its officers.

For information about permission to reproduce selections from this book, write to:

Permissions
Kettering Foundation Press
200 Commons Road
Dayton, Ohio 45459

This book is printed on acid-free paper.
First edition, 2014
Manufactured in the United States of America

ISBN: 978-0-923993-53-5
Library of Congress Control Number: 2013955704

CONTENTS

DEDICATION

THIS BOOK IS AN EXAMPLE of maximum feasible peer review, and it's dedicated to all the reviewers.

My colleagues at the Kettering Foundation read and commented on innumerable drafts. So did the foundation's associates, research deputies, and research assistants. I would guess that the manuscript had close to a hundred handprints on it before it left our building. In addition, the last draft was reviewed by more than a hundred other people who gave us much of the information used in the book. The book is both about them and for them.

I wish I could say that I took full advantage of all the reviewers' good advice. Regrettably, I didn't. Yet the book profited greatly from what I learned from their comments, even if I failed to take every suggestion.

Sandy decided the remedy wasn't in the schools but in the community, yet she wasn't sure what she could do in the face of what appeared to be widespread indifference.

She sensed that the indifference was a symptom of a deeper problem: the public had become disconnected from the public school. When they drove by the building, they would call it *the* school, not *our* school. Sandy saw her job as rebuilding a sense of ownership.[3] However, she realized she couldn't start with the school and its problems. She had to begin with the things everyone, not just parents, really cared about. Many were concerned that young people were having trouble finding jobs, and, with nothing to do, were getting into trouble. So, Sandy decided to start with people's concerns about both their future and the future of the next generation. She went from being a teacher to being a community builder, which meant creating a citizens' coalition to combat some of the problems in the community that were spilling over into the schools. Curbing alcohol abuse was the coalition's first issue.

Max, a public health professional, was dismayed by the political polarization that quickly stymied his agency's efforts to deal with sensitive issues like reducing pollution and creating landfills for garbage. Unresolved, these problems ended up in the courts, and delays there meant that health hazards went unattended while lawyers wrangled. Max decided that the only way to break the logjams was to go to the people before the polarization set in. But how? Nothing in his training or career provided an answer.

Then Max realized that issues were seldom described in ways that resonated with people's deepest concerns. The descriptions coming from his agency were usually highly technical. Water quality reports, for example, listed possible contaminants by their scientific names and their presence by parts per million. People wondered what all the numbers meant. Furthermore, the options for solving problems quickly became polar opposites—add fluoride to the water or ban all additives. Maybe these ways of identifying and presenting issues were contributing to the divisiveness. Max began working with his community to rename issues to include more than just technical data and to lay out a wider ranger of options to consider. He started holding community forums that changed the way his agency related to the public.

From a Typical Water Quality Report[4]

Regulated Substance	Highest Level Allowed (MCL)	Ideal Goals (MCLG)	Highest Level Detected
Regulated at the Treatment Plant			
Flouride (ppm)	4	4	1.19
Nitrate (ppm)	10	10	1.87
Turbidity (NTU)	TT=1	N/A	0.17
	TT: ≥ 95% must be ≤ 0.3		100%
Cis-1, 2- dichloroethylene (ppb)	70	70	.53
Total Organic Carbon (TOC)	TT	N/A	1.0 ppm
Toluene	1	1	0.62

Sue admitted, with considerable anguish, that her community spent a good deal of time "recovering," as she put it, from the last round of supposed solutions to local problems. The solutions weren't really solutions; they didn't hold long enough to counter persistent difficulties. The problems kept coming back: crime, economic reversals, tornados. In fact, these problems didn't have solutions, but they could be managed.

Local, state, and federal agencies had programs to help and were of some benefit. Yet the problems facing the community had a human side and couldn't be solved without assistance coming from citizens working with other citizens. "Programs don't solve our most serious problems," one minister in Sue's community said, "only people can." He may have had in mind the epidemic of drug abuse that was sweeping over the community.

Sue thought her fellow citizens failed to recognize and commit resources they controlled, which could be used to combat local problems. For example, one of the neighborhoods wracked by joblessness and deteriorating homes wanted to protect its children. Yet even though citizens had opportunities to work with young people in their churches, businesses, and civic organizations, they decided to turn troubled youngsters over to the city's social services department. Certainly the department could help; still, Sue was convinced that families, churches, and even businesses had many of the resources that were needed. She set out to identify these assets and encourage those who had them to put them to use.

Citizens like Sue, Max, and Sandy do useful work, but I don't want to give the impression they are civic saints. Citizens who solve problems aren't all self-sacrificing altruists. And they aren't always right or successful. They can and do fail. They also aren't immune from the concerns, doubts, and even cynicism that affect other people. Nonetheless, they are determined to make their communities better.

By shining a spotlight on these individuals, I am not saying that only certain people are citizens and others aren't. I believe most everyone plays a role as citizen sometimes—even when they don't think what they are doing is citizenship. An act of citizenship can be as simple as voicing an opinion about a problem that affects everyone.

OPERATING THROUGH NETWORKS

After completing these sketches of citizens, I realized I had left out their most important characteristic. "Fixers" don't work alone; they are enmeshed in any number of overlapping networks of people. Their networks are sources of civic energy for getting things done in their communities and organizations.

Like Gene, my cousin Bumpy is a consummate networker. A retired educator in her youthful eighties, she lives in, draws energy from, and adds energy to a host of networks in our hometown. She is a member of the congregation of the Methodist church, the alumni association of the public school, the hospital auxiliary, her bridge club, the county historical society, the cemetery association—just to name some of her connections, which also include our extended family.

All of the citizens I have described need to be seen in this larger context. Otherwise, accounts of their contributions reinforce the familiar "great man" or "great woman" narrative, which give the impression that only extraordinary people produce extraordinary results. Of course, and fortunately, we benefit from exceptional citizens who go above and beyond the call of duty. Yet what they do is so impressive it could overshadow the importance of the networks that allow them to be effective.

This book isn't about extraordinary people; it is about the extraordinary potential in civic relationships, which all of us can create, even with strangers. Civic connections can extend to those who aren't like us and may not particularly like us. We need these people if we are to solve our common problems.

I recall a community that was having terrible difficulties: the economy was stagnant, race relations were strained, the schools were below par. The situation didn't change until a small group of citizens, not a charismatic leader, began to ask who wasn't present when community problems were being discussed—yet needed to be there if the problems were going to be solved. That question led the group to a surprising conclusion: the person they needed most wasn't the mayor or the leading business owner. It was the S.O.B. down the street—the person who wasn't like them and certainly didn't like them. Why weren't this malcontent and other outsiders included in the community discussions? No one invited them. If they had been invited, would they have come? Probably not. So the members of the small group began looking at what discussions the S.O.B.s were in and how the S.O.B.s might join them. That's when the community began to change.

Civic relationships aren't just with friends and neighbors; they are the pragmatic working relationships we create with anyone who is needed in order to solve the problems that threaten everyone's well-being.

COMBATING THE PROBLEMS-BEHIND-THE-PROBLEMS

The citizens I introduced have been called the "real fixers," but they aren't interested in quick fixes. They deal with obvious problems: failing schools (Sandy), disagreements over protecting the environment (Max), and youth-at-risk (Sue). However, they sense that more fundamental and systemic problems are behind the obvious ones and that these have to be dealt with. Otherwise, all of their efforts would just treat symptoms.

Americans are quite aware of problems *in* our democracy because they hit us in the face every day: mortgage foreclosures, the high price of medical care (especially the little pills that cost big bucks), the factory that had been in the community forever but is being dismantled to go overseas. We may suspect that there is more to these problems than meets the eye, although we aren't sure what it is.

Behind the obvious difficulties are often more basic problems that cripple our ability to respond. I would call these problems *of* democracy itself. Like the pollution that kills the microorganisms of a pond or bay, they foul the inner workings of democracy. These systemic problems are different from the circumstantial difficulties that affect all countries, democratic or not. Take worldwide economic recessions; these hit nearly every nation regardless of its political system. Recessions are unquestionably serious, yet they aren't the same as the root problems of democracies, malfunctions in the political system that interfere with responding to disasters like recessions.

Look at the problem-behind-the-problem that Sandy encountered. While failing schools are a terrible problem in any community, improving them is often blocked by a problem *of* democracy. In Sandy's hometown, there wasn't a sufficient public with ownership of the public schools.

Why is that a problem of democracy? Historically, schools have been one of the citizenry's principal engines for democratic progress. Citizens used them to change a colonial system into one that promoted both individual freedom and social stability.[5] When people lose ownership of the schools, they lose some of their ability to shape their future. That's a problem of democracy.

Max sensed that another problem of democracy was behind the divisiveness that was hamstringing his public health department. The problem was in the way issues were being presented to the public. This blocked the thoughtful decision making that is needed to reach sound judgment and come to a pragmatic resolution of differences.

Sue also saw a problem of democracy in her community. It was a lack of what scholars call "political agency or efficacy." People didn't think they had the resources or power within themselves to make a difference.

The problems of democracy that Sue, Max, and Sandy encountered are only three of the systemic problems that prevent democracy from working as it should. The next chapter identifies seven of these problems-behind-the-problems, and they are used as reference points throughout the text.

Frankly, systemic problems aren't always very eye-catching. They don't provoke the emotional reaction that problems in democracy do. Laid off and no job prospects! Homes lost; couldn't pay the mortgages! Children going to school hungry! Those are the issues that get our blood boiling. Underlying problems, on the other hand, may lack this visceral oomph. Nonetheless, the less obvious problems-behind-the-problems cripple a democratic system and its ability to respond to the more visible, in-your-face problems.

PART I
DEMOCRACY RECONSIDERED

1
SYSTEMIC PROBLEMS OF SELF-RULE

THE FIRST OF THE SYSTEMIC PROBLEMS of democracy I put on my list strikes at the heart of democracy: citizens aren't engaged; they are on the sidelines. People are reluctant to get involved in either conventional electoral politics or even civic efforts with other citizens. An example: the low turnout at the polls. Another example: the community projects that fail because citizens—except for the usual suspects—don't show up to do the work. Maybe people don't see their concerns or what is most valuable to them being addressed. Maybe there is little space for them to reason together without expectations of a predetermined conclusion. Maybe the political system has pushed them to the sidelines by gerrymandering their voting precincts so their ballots don't really count. Maybe they've sidelined themselves by retreating to small enclaves out of frustration or cynicism. Whatever the cause, the absence of people who think of themselves as citizens is a serious problem of democracy.

> *Politics ought to be the part-time profession of every citizen.*
> —Dwight D. Eisenhower[1]

The second problem comes on the heels of the first. Issues are approached and discussed in ways that promote divisiveness. Maybe not all of the options for solving the problem are considered. Or only two options, which are polar opposites, are addressed, which leads to an unproductive debate. At the other extreme, the inevitable tensions among options and the necessity for trade-offs are never recognized. Fear of disagreement produces bland discussions.

The third problem follows suit: people may get involved yet make very poor decisions about what they should do or which policies are in their best interest. Hasty reactions fueled by misinformation and emotional biases rule the day. Morally charged disagreements aren't worked through—as, for example, disagreements over what is *right* or *just* when scarce resources for things like health care are to be distributed. This lack of sound public judgment is another serious problem of democracy.

A fourth systemic problem has to do with citizens' perception that they can't really make a difference in politics because they don't have the necessary resources. However, certain kinds of in-your-face problems can only be solved if the citizenry acts. An example: issues involving keeping young people out of harm's way. Institutions like schools and social service agencies are essential, yet they can't do the job alone.

Fifth, citizens may act, but their efforts go in so many different directions that they are ineffective; they aren't mutually supportive. The standard remedy for this lack of coordination can be equally debilitating: a central agency is put in charge and creates burdensome rules and regulations that drain the energy out of citizens' initiatives. This can happen following natural disasters when the spontaneous actions of volunteers fail to mesh with the efforts of professional "first responders." When there is no shared sense of purpose for citizens' initiatives or when bureaucratic control takes away people's control, democratic self-organizing is undermined. That, too, belongs on the list of systemic problems.

Democracies have to respond to ever-changing circumstances, on the one hand, and to difficulties that never seem to go away, on the other. In fact, the problems of democracy are perennial because they are rooted in the human condition. We are always prone to try to get off the field and onto the sidelines, to make poor decisions, to underestimate or overestimate our resources. We can't declare victory and go home where democracy is concerned. To keep up the necessary momentum for dealing with systemic problems, democracies depend on constant collective learning, which promotes both experimentation and persistence. Consequently the sixth problem, the absence of shared learning, keeps democracy from working.

Finally, the seventh problem on my list has been quite acute for some time. It is the mutual distrust that burdens the relationship between citizens and most major institutions, governmental as well as nongovernmental. Institutions doubt that citizens are responsible and capable. And citizens see institutions as unresponsive as well as ineffective.

Democratic politics is both pragmatic and creative. People want to be able to shape their future, that is, to fashion the communities and world in which they live.

2
STRUGGLING FOR
A CITIZEN-CENTERED
DEMOCRACY

THE PROBLEMS-BEHIND-THE-PROBLEMS of democracy can't be solved without citizens. But exactly what role are citizens supposed to play? Is being voters, taxpayers, or volunteers enough? That all depends on what kind of democracy you have in mind.

The democracy discussed on these pages is based on the concepts captured in the two roots of the word itself—*demo* and *cracy*. The *demos* is the citizenry, and the *cracy* (from *kratos*) is their power to rule or prevail. In other words, democracy is governance based on the power of people to shape their future. Citizens are at the center, although it has always been a struggle to keep them there.[2]

The conventional understanding of democracy is as a system of representative government created through contested elections. Representative government is essential, yet I believe it rests on a foundation of a citizenry that does more than vote to choose political leaders. I'm not talking about direct referendum democracy, but rather a democracy of citizens working with citizens to solve common problems and produce things that benefit everyone—things that also help the institutions of representative government work effectively. For a democracy to be strong and resilient, citizens have to be producers, not just consumers.

Some of our nation's founders, however, did not want a democracy and said so emphatically; they wanted a republic of representative

©Anthony Baggett/Dreamstime.com

With public sentiment, nothing can fail;
without it nothing can succeed.

—Abraham Lincoln[1]

government. They were afraid that power in the hands of citizens, particularly the poor, would result in redistributing wealth. Nonetheless, a citizen-centered democracy began to take shape in the town meetings of colonial New England, and then gained strength in the armies of citizens who flocked to the Revolution. As the 18th century gave way to the 19th, citizens took on new roles in settling frontier communities. They built our early churches, schools, roads, and libraries. They organized associations to help their neighbors and assisted those visited by misfortune. They got their hands dirty doing the work required to make things that benefited everyone.[3]

You may remember (because he is cited so often) Alexis de Tocqueville, the French observer, who noted that when Americans faced a problem, they, unlike Europeans, were more likely to turn to their neighbors than to city hall or the statehouse.[4] The citizens Tocqueville wrote about are the political ancestors of the active citizens I introduced in the opening pages of this book. These Americans worry about their role in today's democracy and about the institutions they created to serve them.

DISTRUST THAT'S MUTUAL

Americans know something is wrong with our democracy, and we are concerned about what lies ahead for the country. A 2011 Rasmussen poll showed that more than half of American voters felt the nation's best days were already in the past, and only 17 percent believed the country was heading in the right direction. Granted, people have been pessimistic before, and our confidence in government rises and falls; still, it has remained low for some 40 years. And the government isn't the only institution that has lost the public's confidence. Most major institutions, from the schools to the media, have dropped in the public's esteem.[5] To make matters more serious, this distrust is mutual. Officials in our major institutions often have a low opinion of citizens.

A former mayor of Muncie, Indiana, lost reelection after campaign promises to bring new jobs didn't meet voters' expectations. The *National Journal* quoted her as saying, "Why wasn't I more honest with voters? They didn't want to hear it."[6] She didn't trust the voters and ran what she confessed was a less-than-upright campaign.

This mutual distrust has increased significantly over the last decade. Banks suffered a 24 percent decline in trust between 2002 and 2011. Confidence in the Presidency dropped 23 percent. Even confidence in the Supreme Court has fallen by 13 percent.[7] One reason for the decline, the *National Journal* argues, is the inability of institutions to respond to people's concerns. "It's not just that the institutions

are corrupt or broken; those clichés oversimplify an existential problem: With few notable exceptions, the nation's onetime social pillars
are ill-equipped for the 21st century. Most critically, they are failing
to adapt quickly enough for a population buffeted by wrenching economic, technological, and demographic change."[8] I would add another
reason—people don't feel they have sufficient control over our major
institutions.

The political system, blocked by hyperpolarization that is fueled
by incivility, appears more concerned with which side wins than
with solving problems. People say that voters don't vote, money does.
Interest groups appear to control everything. Politicians seem easily
corrupted. People complain, but some feel they get what they deserve.
Or perhaps the media are to blame. The litany of charges goes on.

> *As it enters the twenty-first century, the United States is*
> *not fundamentally a weak economy, or a decadent society.*
> *But it has developed a highly dysfunctional politics.*
> —Fareed Zakaria[9]

America's leaders are said to be out of touch with what life is like for
most people. In the lines of the old country song, citizens are saying, in
effect, to these leaders, "I don't see me in your eyes anymore." A woman
in Alabama explained, "I think [politicians] all have a personal agenda
and they're not listening to what the average American has to say to
them." While public criticism seems to focus solely on national elected
and political leaders, people are often equally dissatisfied with local
leaders. A woman in New Mexico had in mind local political leaders
and officials when she lamented, "I don't see them calling you back . . .
I can't even get somebody to get us a recycle bin at our school to call us
back."[10] Dan Yankelovich, one of America's premier analysts of public
attitudes, has found that leaders and the public typically come at issues
from vastly different starting points. Their assumptions, definitions,
and expectations are often worlds apart.[11]

Personally, I get uneasy about the popular tendency to demonize politicians and officials of government. But I am reporting what people say, not what I wish they would say. I was never a politician, although I have been an official in government, where I met any number of able, responsible bureaucrats, along with decent, conscientious political leaders committed to serving the public good as they saw it.

STRONGER HANDS, OUR HANDS

With distrust so prevalent, many people feel about politics the way they feel when the remote to their TV set no longer controls the screen. The battery seems to be dead or some kind of bug has invaded the electronics. You can hear their frustration with politics in comments like, "The system is out of whack." "The rules have changed (and I don't know what they are anymore)." Anxious Americans want more control in their own hands, not exclusively in the hands of those who say they will take care of the problems for them.[12] This reassurance isn't reassuring.

Jean Johnson, reporting on research by Public Agenda, describes a discussion where citizens talked at length about unresponsive government, mortgage defaults, and the banking crisis, as well as an apparent lack of accountability and responsibility among leaders. When asked what would help, Jean wrote, people "immediately started talking about citizens taking a stronger role," although many were unsure of what a more robust role would be.[13] The people Public Agenda heard from believed that the only way the country could overcome its current problems is for "average citizens to be less passive and get more involved."[14] People advised one another, "Have the confidence to believe that you can make a change. Don't be defeated before you try."

Illustration by Jennifer Berman

We are the ones we have been waiting for.[15]

The advice to keep trying can be quite persuasive. One study showed that between 2008 and 2010, a majority of Americans were active "in working with others to improve their communities" despite whatever reservations they had about making a difference.[16]

Even though worried and anxious, we Americans still have high expectations for the country. We want to live where justice reigns, where peace is the norm not the exception, and where people are free to follow their conscience. And we want the world our children inherit to be better than the world we have now. Americans have been hopeful for most of our country's 200-plus years and, deep down, many still are.[17]

HOPING TO HOPE

Although people want to hope, hope is fragile. Researchers, drawing from interviews with people from across the country, heard a man from Minnesota saying optimistically, "I think there's a hunger for engagement, generally, with people, and I think they're just looking for ways to be engaged." Less optimistic, a woman from Idaho countered, "When I told the citizens I was supposed to work with that they . . . have more power than [they] believed, I think I believed it when I said it. And I believed it all the times that I've lived it. But I'm not sure it's as true as it used to be." As though trying to reconcile these two perceptions, a woman from Rhode Island reasoned that, "when I talk to people, they do care; they just don't know what to do with themselves."[18]

Americans haven't given up on the country; they think we have the DNA for resilience in our bones. Many believe, however, that we have lost our way because we've misplaced our moral compass. Americans seem to some to be irrepressible shoppers who have been taken over by consumerism and materialism. Wall Street is a convenient symbol for the greed people see everywhere. Research by the Harwood Institute for Public Innovation found citizens want a moral order that values honesty, punishes greed, and rewards social responsibility.[19]

> Hearing the comments of various people gives a sense that citizens are ambivalent or confused. A better reading of what they are saying may be that people have a range of many hopes and fears that they are trying to balance. This gives any account of what they are saying an "on the one hand, but on the other . . ." tone. Although this makes for an uneven, halting description, it is actually a better reflection of the public mind.

While proudly independent, Americans also know that they can only survive by working together. People recall old sayings like you have to "give a little to get a little."[20] Many also think that citizens have too little compassion for one another; too little respect, too little regard for the dignity of others.

Starting Where We Are

When it comes to realizing our dreams for our country, grand visions and all-encompassing reforms don't seem as credible as small projects where citizens take responsibility, decide on what should be done, and do much of the work themselves. Homegrown change is appealing because it is authentic. Unsure that they can trust large institutions, people look to their fellow citizens to fix what is out of whack through joint efforts that build confidence. Neighbors coming together to paint a school isn't important just because the school building will be more attractive; the painting is valued as a demonstration of what can be accomplished when citizens work together.[21]

In this study of public attitudes, Rich Harwood found that "the task, as people see it, is to kick-start a new trajectory where actions start small and local, between and among people; where clear goals are set and achieved, and where people can restore faith in themselves and one another and in the belief that Americans still can get things done *together*." He quotes a Dallas woman who said that people can't wait for others to act on their behalf. Initiative is key. "If the change is going to happen," she said, "it's going to be grass roots. We're going to have to spur that movement and keep it going." And a woman from Denver suggested, "Just start small!" Another in Detroit talked about the importance of hands-on democracy: "If more people . . . are more hands on in the community, then it's going to eventually lead to better opportunities."[22]

Harwood sees a connection between local issues and national resilience. "The people we met," he reports, "believe the country faces enormous challenges that require significant action. The purpose of starting small and starting local, and . . . meeting one achievable goal after another, is to rebuild the confidence and sense of common purpose in the nation."[23]

But what about global problems? Those who believe in starting small say that, without a sense of efficacy and shared purpose, people won't be able to tackle larger problems. And they point out that local efforts can and do build to form larger movements.

As I will explain later in more detail, there are opportunities in everyday life to demonstrate what citizens can do—opportunities for people to exercise more control. Unfortunately, these opportunities are often overlooked because they are obscured by the dominant understanding of politics as something only politicians do through governments. If what citizens do isn't related directly to elections or governments, the conventional wisdom says it couldn't possibly be politics. Failing to recognize the politics of citizens working with citizens contributes to people's sense that they can't make a difference.

THE POLITICS PEOPLE DON'T CALL POLITICS

I'm not saying that elections and governments are unimportant or that citizens can run the country by ourselves. That would be ridiculous. What I am saying is that our political system operates in two spheres that are interrelated. The obvious sphere, the one we associate with politics, is dominated by dramatic elections and titanic struggles in government. It's run by large institutions through laws, regulations, and policies. The less obvious arena of politics, the politics of citizens, doesn't even have a commonly accepted name. People won't even call it politics.

Philosophers have helped make the less obvious politics visible by writing about "the political," meaning the part of our lives that we share with other people, which isn't confined to what we do as voters and taxpayers.[24] Other scholars use terms like public or civic life to describe "the political." The phrase with the greatest attraction recently has been "civil society," the society that citizens create through the things they do with other citizens. I prefer terms like "citizen-centered democracy" or, more succinctly, "citizen politics" because the words reclaim a vocabulary that people rightfully own.

The politics I am talking about is Sandy and her community taking more responsibility for the education of the next generation. It's the people in Max's forum facing difficult decisions about protecting the environment while growing the economy. It's Sue and her neighbors using local resources to combat local problems. This politics is deeply rooted in everyday life and personal experience, and it thrives in places not normally associated with politics—over lunch counters, at coffee shops, in carpools, and waiting in checkout lines.[25]

> An African once told me that in his country people rarely talk about politics; they are afraid. Yet, in the marketplaces, he said, they talk about running the village schools and coping with droughts. They didn't think of these conversations as "political," but he did.

The politics that citizens create is difficult to recognize for what it is, so much so that it almost seems to be America's secret political life. When people do recognize it and realize it is no secret at all but something that happens every day, the insight changes their picture of the political world. They see ways for citizens to make a difference, possibilities they hadn't noticed before. This insight doesn't come from reading paragraphs like this one, however. It comes from the experience of *doing* the work of citizens.

If everyday politics is a secret, it's an open one. It lives today through thousands of citizen initiatives in ad hoc associations for removing litter from public roads, protecting the environment, and keeping drunk drivers off the highways.

Civic Renewal

Despite citizens' frustrations, despite the downdrafts of cynicism and hopelessness, and despite the forces that push people to the sidelines, there have been so many citizen initiatives in recent years that some scholars believe the country is experiencing a civic renewal movement. Albeit this movement is inspired by a variety of causes, which may be expected in a democracy, the overall aim is to put citizens back in the center of our democracy.

Politics with citizens at the center is creating its own literature.

Ben Barber has called this politics "strong democracy" in a book by that title. Ben's book can be read as a companion to Harry Boyte's *The Backyard Revolution*. Although written some time ago, this literature contains ideas that continue to resonate. More recently, we've seen case studies of numerous civic initiatives—some with bold headlines announcing *The Next Form of Democracy* (by Matt Leighninger) and others expanding the definition of democracy, as in Mark Warren's paper on "a problem-based approach to democratic systems."[26]

Civic renewal is also discussed in *Civic Innovation in America* by Carmen Sirianni and Lewis Friedland and in Peter Levine's *We Are the Ones We Have Been Waiting For*. These are only a few of the many books in a growing literature on citizen politics. While this is not the place to list all the books, I would add Xavier de Souza Briggs' *Democracy as Problem Solving*.[27]

> While I agree that democracy has to do with overcoming problems, I don't think everything in democratic politics is directly related to problem solving. That would make democracy too instrumental. Democracy is about transformation, not just transaction.[28]

The work that citizens do with citizens is, at its core, the work of creating things essential to combating problems. Where is the work done? Briggs believes that the community is the primary collective in deciding and acting, not because all the needed resources are local, but because "societies cannot do without effective local systems for acting on public problems." Briggs also makes a helpful distinction between various kinds of civic strategies based on whether they reflect a concept of democracy that is broader than just expanding the voice of citizens and holding meetings to engage people.[29] Unfortunately, America's civic capacities often go unrecognized or undervalued. And I am pleased to find studies showing how important those capacities are. Most notably, Elinor Ostrom, who won the Nobel Prize in Economic Sciences in 2009, demonstrated that the work done by citizens is essential in sustaining the equitable management of common resources.[30]

In the 1990s, I wrote about citizen politics in *Politics for People*. And I have been pleased to see that what were then novel insights in the literature about democracy are now regularly acknowledged in more recent books and articles. For example, Bob Putnam's argument that "civil society" is crucial to democracy is now generally accepted.[31] The same is true of concepts of power. The notion that power isn't just in authority *over* others but also in the relationships citizens form with other citizens is widespread. Perhaps most far-reaching of this rethinking, questions are now being raised about the knowledge citizens use in politics. For instance, Ostrom found that the knowledge citizens have of local conditions is sometimes superior to expert knowledge. Even though expert or scientific facts still sit atop the pyramid of knowledge, more arguments are being made that citizens have other equally valid ways of knowing, especially when making judgments about political issues.

I am not assuming, nor does the literature I've cited assume, that the work citizens do is all-powerful—able to defeat vested interests, overcome global economic tsunamis, solve every community problem, or transform every institution. Citizens trying to make a difference face a host of obstacles. Those who involve others find it takes time and raises red flags for critics who doubt the competence and judgment of people. And people trying to reach out to institutional officials can be frustrated by indifference, outright resistance, and, sometimes, reasonable caution.

To be fair, trained professionals and officials, for their part, may have reason to be wary of what untrained volunteers will do without time-consuming supervision. Deputizing civic groups to carry out programs can lead to problems when informal civic associations ignore or fail to recognize legal constraints. Financial mismanagement can be a problem, too.

Institutional officers trying to engage citizens are also often frustrated by what appears to be the citizenry's lack of response to overtures to participate. And they may be stung by the complaints they get from their colleagues for trying to involve people. Furthermore, despite all kinds of metrics that institutions use to "prove" officeholders are doing a good job, citizens remain unconvinced, which is another source of officeholders' frustration.

POLITICAL ENVIRONMENTALISM

Admittedly, what citizens do by working with other citizens may make only small, incremental differences, yet these small changes have given us much of what we value in life. As I've reported, the change might begin with nothing more than neighbors coming together to create a community garden or to restore a local park. Still, doing something to improve a neighborhood can be an antidote to the cynicism and hopelessness that is guaranteed to disempower people. Working together builds a sense of possibility and responsibility.

Take the case of Tupelo, Mississippi. Tupelo changed itself from being the poorest town in the poorest county in the poorest state, to become a model of economic and social progress. The change was precipitated by people in the rural neighborhoods around Tupelo meeting to decide on something they could do themselves to make life better—and then doing it. That eventually changed the political environment and spread throughout the region. This remarkable story is captured in a study done by a scholar, Vaughn Grisham, who watched it happen.[32]

Like Sandy, Max, and Sue, the people who began doing civic work in the rural neighborhoods around Tupelo could be described as political environmentalists because of where they have found the resources for their work.[33] What they needed to get started came from the skills and experiences of their fellow citizens, from the ties citizens had with one another, and from people's inherent ways of knowing, deciding, and acting.[34] These resources were all in their political environment.

THE WORK OF DEMOCRACY IS WORK

The message here and throughout this book is that citizens can make a difference by joining to make things that help solve common problems. That is the way people empower themselves—through civic work. Edgar Cahn said the same thing more pointedly: "The work of democracy *is* work."

The work citizens do is hard, prone to setbacks and delays. It is done incrementally, and seldom produces big headlines or wins awards. Still, it is empowering because it puts more control in the hands of people.

To elaborate: citizens generate the power they need to make a difference through the collective decision making that goes with collective action. Collective deciding and acting is work, and this work produces things that serve the good of all—a new playground to get kids off the streets, homes for the homeless. This is how citizens become more than constituents, consumers, voters, and taxpayers; they become producers. And they aren't defined just by their relationship to the state or government; they are defined first by their relationship to other citizens.

I also want to emphasize that democratic civic work isn't done by following a formula or employing some technique. The work moves forward by people constantly learning together. I should write this in bold capitals: **LEARNING TOGETHER**. The constancy, the persistence, in civic work comes from communities learning how to fail *successfully*. Learning together or "public learning" is key.

> *How to fail intelligently . . . is one of the greatest*
> *arts in the world.*
>
> —Charles F. Kettering[35]

In the work citizens do, learning and doing are combined. That is, the work doesn't just accomplish specific tasks, like hammering nails to join boards. The work prompts citizens to make discoveries, discoveries that reveal possibilities and resources that haven't been fully utilized. *The work is both doing and learning, and the learning is in the doing.*

POSSIBILITIES NOT PROOFS

While this book is written for anyone who wants to make the differ-ence that citizens should make, it isn't full of answers, nor does it have a list of techniques guaranteed to bring success. There are no case studies proving what will work. There aren't any formulas, best practices to fol-low, or lofty appeals to people's better angels. The book offers different ways to think about politics, citizens, and the problems-behind-the-problems of democracy. That is, the book doesn't make claims based on proofs and doesn't have "findings" in the academic sense. Rather, it offers insights or provides lenses for seeing what is already happening that point to unrealized possibilities.

You may wonder if what you are reading can fit into your realities. Is it practical? Can it be applied? Would you have to change everything you are doing?

How the insights in this book are applied in practical situations depends on local conditions and circumstances. No one is familiar with every community or all the challenges that other organizations face, and applying any new perspective usually requires trial-and-error experiments. The research reported here suggests that communities and organizations can find many of their own answers in the way they go about learning from these experiments.

The Kettering Foundation, which gathered the research for this book, is a nonpartisan, nongovernmental, nonprofit organization and not a grantmaker. The foundation's research comes primarily from people and organizations experimenting to find better ways of com-bating the systemic problems-behind-the-problems of democracy. These groups provide Kettering with accounts of their experiences in exchange for insights the foundation has gained from past accounts of similar experiences. The foundation collects these different experi-ences and then combines them, weaving parts together to illustrate an idea in a practical way. The stories are just that—stories; they aren't social science case studies.

In these exchanges, while participants don't get answers or new techniques, they can get a different set of lenses for seeing themselves and the problems they face. Different perspectives are often the key to more effective work and problem solving. The exchanges allow participants, including those from the foundation, to discover new people and new ideas, and these discoveries make it possible for participants to rediscover themselves, which is a kind of learning. The book is also based on studies done by and for the foundation and on related research by scholars, many of whom are associated with the foundation. The purpose of all this research is to learn what it takes to make a democracy work as it *should*. "Should" acknowledges that how democracy works is a normative question; no one has the right answer. That has to be determined by the *demos*, by the citizenry. This means that democracy (at least the kind the foundation studies) requires collective responsibility, which can't be exported or imported. It has to come from within.

Although this book is about the United States, Kettering has had the privilege of learning from active citizens in many other countries—from nearby Cuba to faraway South Africa, from Russian villages in the North to Australia and New Zealand in the South.

To be sure, few of those the foundation has heard from thought that what they were doing was an "experiment." That's Kettering's terminology. But when citizens deal with the problems-behind-the-problems, it certainly takes them into unfamiliar terrain with no instructions to follow. They have to improvise. Drawing from "their experiments," the foundation has identified opportunities in the ordinary routines of everyday life where the citizenry can regain the control people feel they have lost.

I want to emphasize that in its research the foundation is continually learning; its studies are never finished. Since learning is critical to democracy and key to a community's ability to solve problems, the foundation tries to operate in a learning mode itself.

3
THE POLITICAL ECOSYSTEM

THE POLITICAL ENVIRONMENT includes both what citizens do with citizens and what institutions do, because the two are interdependent. Political life usually begins locally and small: that is, in neighborhoods, in informal associations, and around kitchen tables. This is where the first opportunities to make a difference are. Then institutions like representative assemblies, government agencies, and nongovernmental organizations (NGOs) bring other resources to bear.

Citizens and institutions interacting in a political environment make me think of the natural ecological system. I find that a useful analogy, and I mean it only as an analogy. To be sure, a case can be made that politics is actually like the complex adaptive systems found in nature.[1] However, I use the analogy to provide a broader frame of reference for thinking about politics, and not everything I report will relate back to an ecology.

I would also add that by saying the political system is like an ecosystem, I am not implying that an ecosystem is a perfect state of nature. I am just referring to what goes on every day in the political environment, which is both good and bad.

When I think about an ecosystem, I have in mind the Gulf Coast because I grew up nearby. Governments, schools, and other established institutions could be roughly analogous to oil rigs, docks, and large buildings on the shore. The things citizens do and the associations among them might be thought of as something like barrier islands and all that happens in the marshes of the wetlands.

The ecological context helps to see politics as more than what happens in elections and governments—without ignoring the importance of either. The analogy simply distinguishes the things that citizens do with citizens, which are often informal or organic, from the things that politicians and government officials do, which are usually formal or institutional.

We already know a great deal about elections and governments, so I am going to concentrate on citizen-to-citizen politics. But I am also going to talk about the relationship of civic life to what happens in formal, institutional politics. The political ecosystem has two components, and the connection between them is absolutely crucial.

While different, organic and institutional politics are profoundly interdependent. The connection of organic and institutional spheres is obvious on the Gulf. Large structures like oil rigs and docks are affected by what happens on barrier islands and in salt marshes and vice versa. This was obvious when a drilling rig on the Gulf Coast exploded in 2010, sending millions of gallons of oil into the wetlands. And it was obvious when the lack of natural barriers exposed New Orleans and its institutions to the full fury of Hurricane Katrina.[2]

THE WETLANDS: BENEFICIAL— AND DANGEROUS

Today, everyone rushes to protect the coastal wetlands when there is an oil spill, even though we once overlooked the value of what goes on in these swampy areas. For years, we filled in the marshes, and the sea life that bred in the wetlands died. We removed barrier islands to make better shipping channels and unintentionally made better hurricane channels. We learned the important role that nature's wetlands play the hard way.

In pointing out the crucial role the wetlands play, I want to emphasize that I am not ignoring their dangers. Some of what happens in swamps can be downright dangerous. And, as in the natural ecosystem, the political wetlands have the equivalents of poisonous snakes and alligators—prejudices, selfishness, greed, and just plain meanness. The point that I want to make is that not everything that happens in the wetlands is good, and not everything that is institutional is bad. A great many of the problems-behind-the-problems of democracy originate in the darker waters of the wetlands, just as many of the resources for combating these problems are also found there.

As I've said, the importance of the political equivalents of the Gulf Coast's wetlands is prone to be overlooked. Informal gatherings, ad hoc associations, and the seemingly innocuous banter that goes on when people mull over their everyday experiences appear inconsequential when compared with what happens in elections, legislative bodies, and courts. Yet mulling over the meaning of the day's events at bus stops can be the wellspring of public decision making. Connections made in these informal gatherings can become the basis for civic networks, and the ad hoc associations formed there can morph into civic organizations.

Here is an example of the often undocumented civic life, drawn from several reports shared with the foundation: Ernesto was a teacher who lived in a Hispanic community that was seen—and to some extent saw itself—as having no civic life, at least as civic engagement is usually measured.[3] The people were poor; they appeared to be busy just surviving. For most, English was a second language, limiting contact with those who spoke only English. Voter turnout was low. People protested occasionally, though it was usually about a local matter, and the protests seldom made the news.

The U.S. Bureau of Labor Statistics' report on volunteering reinforces this perception of a weak civic life in Ernesto's community. Its 2012 report shows that only 15.2 percent of Hispanics volunteered for "unpaid work . . . through or for an organization," as compared to 27.8 percent of whites and 21.1 percent of African Americans.[4]

When Ernesto realized that his community was seen as having no civic life, he knew it wasn't so. The bureau's statistics didn't surprise him because few people he knew were involved in formal volunteer programs. Yet they would help a neighbor in a heartbeat, just not through formal channels. People were constantly joining together to solve problems and creating things that benefited everyone. They started a community garden on a vacant lot and built a clubhouse where they taught classes, held barbecues, and played music. They seldom held community meetings, yet they talked about political issues over garden plots, at the grocery store, and on the neighborhood street corners. These were issues that affected them personally, like the lack of jobs and what was happening to their children. The kind of civic work that was going on, however, often went unrecognized as such—even by those most engaged in it.

Fortunately, some organizations have recognized that there is a civic life that isn't in the statistics yet is very real. CASA (Court Appointed Special Advocates for Children), for example, has found a rich tradition of involvement in communities like Ernesto's.[5] It just isn't documented.

WHAT THE POLITICAL WETLANDS CONTRIBUTE

The political wetlands hold an array of unique and valuable resources like those Ernesto recognized. Nature's wetlands may look placid, but they are teeming with life. Important work is going on in them; harmful substances are being filtered out, birth and regeneration are everywhere. The same is true of the political wetlands. In them, people practice a politics that is quite different from institutional politics— different in objectives, organization, and methods. That type of politics is what I've called citizen-centered because citizens are defined by their relationships with other citizens, not just their connection to the state. These civic relationships are based on reciprocity—receiving and giving in return. Yet citizen-to-citizen relationships are not the same as those of family and friends. They are pragmatic and work-related. They develop in the situations cited earlier—when citizens coalesce in order to rebuild their community after a disaster, when they organize to construct houses for the homeless, and when they come together with police to keep young people safe.

> *We have an instinct for democracy because we have*
> *an instinct for wholeness; we get wholeness only through*
> *reciprocal relations, through infinitely expanding*
> *reciprocal relations.*
>
> —Mary Parker Follett[6]

The political wetlands also harbor mindsets about how things get done, which influence the way people act. Norms prescribe certain behaviors and proscribe others. (I just mentioned one—reciprocity.) These wetlands are also structured around a multitude of social relationships, some tightly resistant to outsiders and others more open and inclusive. These ways of relating affect what can and can't be done as well as the "costs" of conducting the business of politics (the better the relationships, the lower the costs). The political wetlands affect the way people habitually communicate with one another, which influences the nature of decision making. Who talks to whom about what is significant in politics. And the wetlands develop cultures that determine how well people learn from their experiences and whether they change as their circumstances change.

Political wetlands have their own structures, which I have said are not board tables but kitchen tables; not assemblies like legislative bodies but common gatherings, once in post office lobbies and now on the Internet. These structures are more like sand than concrete. Ad hoc groups and alliances form, then fall away as a project is completed yet reappear when another task is at hand.

At its best, citizen politics in the wetlands is focused on the well-being of communities as a whole and their capacity to overcome adversity—their resilience. This politics involves more than volunteering to serve Thanksgiving dinner at a homeless shelter. It goes deeper than voting, obeying laws, and paying taxes. It includes but goes beyond serving on advisory bodies and participating in government hearings. It is a politics where citizens don't just comply or advise; they act. They get things done. They produce.

In the wetlands, citizen politics operates on a micro level. You might say it is the micropolitics of democracy. The groups that citizens form aren't large and tend to be informal. There may not be a great many of them. Their power, however, lies in the significance of the ideas they generate, the work they do by collective effort, the pervasiveness of their associations, and the hope they generate.

> *Never doubt that a small group of thoughtful, committed*
> *citizens can change the world; indeed, it's the only thing*
> *that ever has.*
>
> —Attributed to Margaret Mead[7]

The insight that politics is like an ecosystem came from the realization that what Kettering was seeing was more political than civil society, yet more civic than grassroots politics.[8] This is not a criticism of either, only a distinction. The ecological and wetlands analogies are better suited to describing what the foundation has been observing.

FROM REFORM TO COLONIZATION

Even though the political wetlands have resources, they also have dangers; so institutions often try to reform or "improve" them. Given the powerful resources and orderly routines of institutions, the wetlands appear not only dangerous but also deficient. So institutions are prone to act *on* the political wetlands rather than in league *with* them. And when institutions concentrate on reforming the wetlands, they miss opportunities for building on the politically regenerative forces that are, in fact, already at work in them.

Institutional reforms tend to colonize the political wetlands, that is, to remake them in the image of the institutions that want to reform them.[9] Sadly, the consequences of these well-intended efforts are often just the opposite of what the reforms set out to do. For instance, when informal wetland associations morph into formal organizations, they may lose the characteristics that made them effective. Associations of neighbors helping neighbors may become rule-bound and less responsive to people's varying circumstances. This has happened in some neighborhood associations that were deputized by local governments to help set budget priorities. They became quasi-official bodies.[10]

The ill effects of colonization on informal civic associations became apparent to some grantmaking foundations when they realized that their grants to solve problems weren't working. In studying why this was happening, the Kettering Foundation noticed that the institutions the grantmakers were funding had different characteristics from those the ad hoc associations' citizens used when they solved problems. In the foundation's report on the findings, the institutions were called "Squares" and the ad hoc civic associations "Blobs" in order to emphasize the difference. Edgar Cahn picked up on this distinction in his book, *No More Throw-Away People*, and turned the foundation's findings into a very clever animation, "The Parable of the Blobs and Squares."[11]

Cahn called institutions like hospitals, universities, community service providers, and volunteer organizations "Squares." He labeled informal affinity groups and grassroots associations as "Blobs":

> The Blobs seemed to have the energy, the vitality, the contacts, the gossip, the networks that were needed to deal with the problems. But the money invariably went to the Squares because the Squares knew how to manage it, account for it, spend it. They had the accountants, the bookkeeping, the tax-exemptions, the equipment, the institutional capacity, the expertise and the presumptive competence.

> The problem was that no matter how much the Squares promised to reach out in the community and get at the root causes of the problems, the Squares never got there. They really weren't able to get to where the problems were or mobilize the energy of the community. A gulf separated the Squares from the Blobs.

The logical response of the foundations was to try to . . . bridge that gulf. So they started funding Partnerships and Collaboratives. In order to get the grants, foundations insisted that the Squares partner with the Blobs. But regardless of the formal partnerships, the Squares kept the money and dominated the scene—throwing a few crumbs to the Blobs, putting a few representatives on the Board, hiring some "natives" as outreach workers. But the partnership approach didn't seem to pay off as a way to capture the energy of the Blobs.

The next step was an obvious one: Give at least some of the money directly to the Blobs to solve the problem. But when that was attempted in the form of grants and sub-contracts, something strange occurred: The Blobs were required to turn into little Squares in order to get the money and account for it. That required a major investment in training and technical assistance. Grass roots groups were taught to develop mission statements and strategic plans in order to remain "true" to mission. Neighborhood leaders were trained in how to be Board members, how to conduct "proper" meetings, how to write and amend by-laws, and what their responsibilities were as Board members. They needed a corporate charter, by-laws, a tax-exempt status, and an adequate accounting system. By the time those groups and those leaders jumped through all those hoops, they had ceased to be Blobs. Handling all the reporting requirements and other accountability demands meant there was no time or energy to be what they had been.[12]

Cahn's parable of the Blobs and Squares is a cautionary tale of what can happen in colonization.[13]

An aside from US history: while Squares have certainly made the Blobs rather "Square-ish," originally *the Blobs created many of the Squares*! Early civic groups often turned to the government to carry out their agendas. Governments responded by creating bureaucracies to implement the programs that the Blobs advocated. And these Squares issued rules and regulations to advance the worthy causes the Blobs championed, which began to make the Blobs "Square-ish." There is little evidence that the influence went in reverse; that the Blobs don't seem to have made the Squares "Blob-ish."[14]

More Unintended Consequences

Another example of the unfortunate effects that institutions can have on the wetlands: initiatives intended to encourage *more* citizen engagement have sometimes decreased participation.[15] Institutions set the terms for participation or decide on the work citizens are to do. As a result, people lose interest because they never really own the work and engagement declines.

Worse than that, institutional efforts to involve citizens sometimes make people mad as the devil. A school board's efforts to engage citizens found the effort actually harmed the board's relationship with the community when board members made a unilateral decision on an issue involving school closure that the board had initially opened up to public participation. Although community forums were held, the board members acted without taking into consideration the public's views. Many citizens were left feeling manipulated.[16]

Institutional engagement efforts to garner support for a school or government agency can also backfire. Getting public support is a necessary and laudable objective, and the strategy is usually to persuade people of the importance of the institution. Yet focusing on connecting people to institutions may overlook the importance of citizens first connecting with one another. Without those connections, the best the engagement strategy can produce is a persuaded population, not the fully engaged and responsible public that institutions need.

Still another example of unintended consequences of institutional interventions in the political wetlands: the pressuring of small, citizen-led projects to get "up to scale" has resulted in people losing some of their control because the expansion usually requires hiring a staff of professional managers who sometimes displace citizens. And copying the "best practices" of purportedly successful participatory models, which institutions also encourage, can have a particularly ironic consequence. Copying encourages imitation rather than innovation.

Most unfortunate of all, when the reforms that institutions promote fail to make use of the meaningful work of citizens, people have less confidence that they can bring about the changes they want. What they are often asked to contribute—hold bake sales or volunteer as aides in schools—doesn't seem to matter much. If people can't find anything meaningful to do, they soon lose interest. In a study by John Gaventa and Gregory Barrett, the authors write, "Participation in formal governance spaces, especially where not backed by collective action, may be linked to a sense of tokenism, or relatively empty forms of participation, which may not contribute by themselves to positive change."[17] However, when citizens are involved in doing something significant, it encourages them to believe that they might make a difference. People don't expect that everything they do will be successful, but improvement at least becomes imaginable.

Why should these misadventures resulting from colonization continue to have such unintended consequences? After all, the consequences are fairly obvious. The Squares know what they are attempting isn't working. Why they persist may have something to do with the internal dynamics and incentives of Squares. Discussions that Rich Harwood and John Creighton had with a representative sample of NGOs uncovered powerful disincentives that kept the Squares and Blobs apart. The Harwood/Creighton report found "a profound and airtight gestalt of inwardness, planning, and professionalism" to be the dominant mentality in the nonprofit world.[18] Even though the Squares (in this case, NGOs) genuinely wanted to work with the Blobs, "they face a series of difficult trade-offs in their core missions, and naturally tend to protect their own interests. The overwhelming central imperative for nonprofit executives is the stability of the organization." Pressure to protect the NGOs puts a premium on "ensuring the survival of the organization and achieving its core objectives before pursuing 'secondary goals,' such as building civic capacity in . . . communities."[19]

This study also found that officers and staff members of the NGOs became more risk averse and less inclined to experiment as their organizations became more inward looking. They saw engaging citizens as high risk, because people are unpredictable and prone to conflict. Outreach initiatives might "backfire."[20]

Furthermore, many of the NGOs in the study were dependent on grants from government agencies and large grantmakers, so they set their agendas to match the agendas of their funders rather than the priorities of the communities they served.

DIFFERENCES THAT MAKE A DIFFERENCE

One of the principal reasons for the colonization of the political wetlands is that it's easy for Squares to miss the differences between the way citizens go about their work and the way institutions do theirs. I can't emphasize the importance of these differences enough; they are subtle, yet profound.

The differences begin in concepts of power. Citizen power isn't the same as institutional power. Earlier I described it as the power people generate through pragmatic working relationships with others. Democratic citizens empower themselves; nobody else does it for them.

Self-government would be impossible if we didn't have power within ourselves as a citizenry. Harry Boyte at the Center for Democracy and Citizenship makes this point by asking an arresting question: "If I empower you, who really has the power?"

Conventional wisdom says that some people have power and some don't. Those who don't are seen—and often see themselves—as powerless. This perception leads to the assumption that those without power can be empowered only by the already powerful. The power that people truly own, however, is generated when their experiences, insights, and talents are combined with the experiences, insights, and talents of others.

Citizens gain power from taking responsibility or ownership of their problems and their actions. If all citizens do is consent to actions taken in their name, "We, the People," the public, will be no more than what I've called a "persuaded populace," which doesn't have the power needed to sustain self-government. Certainly citizens should listen to reasoned arguments and collect information; yet, in the end, they have to make decisions among themselves and act on those decisions. Citizens are more disposed to take ownership of what they have participated in choosing than what has been chosen for them. Being sold on what others have decided doesn't have the same political effect— it doesn't create reservoirs of political will and energy.

The power that comes from people's ability to make things through their relationships with others is what has been described as power *with*. The power of institutions comes largely from their resources and authority. It is power *over*. The more citizens are able to exercise their kind of power, the less they are dependent on institutional power. And institutional power is often more effective if joined by civic power.

The way citizens go about their work empowers them; that is, it gives them a great ability to shape the future. Actually, the tasks that make up the work of both citizens and institutions are much the same. Regardless of who does them, all political tasks have to do with deciding, organizing, and implementing. But *how* citizens go about carrying out these tasks is not at all like the way institutions work.

Illustration by Jennifer Berman

People own what they make more than they
own what has been made for them.

How Citizens Get Things Done

The distinctive way citizens go about their work in the political wetlands
begins in the choice of words used to identify a problem. Although
the names people give to problems may seem insignificant, they can
capture the things people hold dear—their most troubling concerns,
their highest hopes, their deepest fears. These names are rooted in life
at its most basic; they reflect the ends and means of human existence.[21]
The names capture survival imperatives like security from danger. And
they are different from the ones that professionals and politicians use.
For example, citizens want to feel that they are safe in their homes, and
this feeling of security is less quantifiable yet more compelling than the
statistics professionals use to describe crime. When the names given
to problems reflect what people consider valuable, citizens are already

engaged in the politics they don't call politics. They don't have to be enlisted as much as connected.

The knowledge needed to decide what to *do* about problems is also different—as is the way the knowledge is produced. Citizens create their knowledge in a cauldron of acting, reflecting, and deciding in the wetlands. Typically, experts create knowledge through rigorously disciplined science. When citizens produce knowledge, it increases their control.

The differences in the ways decisions are made are also important. If citizens are to make sound decisions, they must look at a range of options, not just one or two, and then weigh the likely consequences of those options against all that is valuable to them. In many ways that is what officials in institutions should do, but the difference is in what people are weighing when they decide. People weigh what they hold dear. These are deeply held concerns that are often intangible, like the feeling of security I just mentioned. Officials in institutions—though influenced by the concerns common to all human beings—are more likely to make decisions using factual information. How much money would be saved if the age for receiving Social Security benefits were changed by one year? By two?

The resources citizens use to do their work are equally distinctive; they include assets found in the political wetlands, which exist in even the poorest communities.[22] Citizens' resources are organic and often intangible, such as commitment and political will or civic energy. These are different from the resources of institutions, which are largely material and technical.

Of course, no decision is self-implementing. Institutions meticulously plan what they will do. (Think of the planning that goes into building a new highway.) Citizens don't implement their decisions that way, but neither can they move forward helter-skelter if they expect to be effective. The variety of ways in which the citizenry acts can be loosely coordinated through a shared sense of direction. This is unlike the actions taken by institutions, which are usually (though not always) uniform and directed by a single plan or central agency.

The commitment of resources to civic action is enforced by covenants or the promises people make to one another. "I will do X, if you will do Y." Institutional commitments, on the other hand, are enforced by legal contracts. Citizen covenant making may sound idealistic, yet it works. Covenants have their own kind of leverage, which is social or peer group pressure.[23] A community leader explained the generally high attendance at his community's meetings this way: If you don't show up, somebody will say something to you about it.

One last but key difference: citizens bring about change voluntarily through collective learning and the innovation it generates. Institutions, such as those of government, bring about change largely through mandating policies, passing laws, and promulgating regulations—along with providing funding.

What Results?

Not only are the ways citizens do their work distinctive, so also are their goals and the results their efforts produce. Harwood research, you will recall, shows that people working together is, itself, an important objective of citizen politics.[24] As one community leader reasoned, "If all the people in the city are banded together to make it a better place to live, then it will be a better place to live."[25]

The more tangible results of the work done by citizens include the creation of a stronger civic architecture in a community—broad-based associations with members who think of themselves as citizens rather than only as representatives of some group or interest. These associations and their networks help span the economic, social, and geographic boundaries that separate people from one another and balkanize society. Networks in the wetlands link various sectors of a community, creating new ties and strengthening norms of cooperation.[26]

In Grand Rapids, Michigan, a retired business executive and a school administrator helped establish a network of more than 30 civic and educational organizations that addressed three issues every year.

Illustration by Jennifer Berman

We've got to do something; we've got to band together.
—Ella Ramirez, citizen

Rather than simply promoting particular projects, their objective was to build more effective working relationships throughout the community. The network itself was a concrete accomplishment, although you wouldn't find it listed in the city directory.

The ultimate result of the work done in the political wetlands is the creation of a democratic public that's more than an electorate, a constituency, or just everybody. It's made of people active in the work of citizens. This public is not reducible to a collection of special interest groups. It's more. It isn't the silent majority or the cadre of volunteers who care for the less fortunate. It's more. It isn't a consensual body but rather a body of civic initiative. It's a citizenry concerned about solving common problems. It's a political community that includes but isn't limited to neighbors and friends. It's a citizenry that holds itself, not just officeholders, responsible. It's a citizenry that owns its problems.

PART II
CITIZENS
AND
COMMUNITIES

4
"HERE, SIR, THE PEOPLE GOVERN."
REALLY?

I'VE SKETCHED OUT THE ROUGH OUTLINES of a case for citizen-centered democracy and suggested that it draws its strength from the political wetlands, where there are often unrecognized but substantial resources for people to use in the work citizens must do to empower themselves. In making this case, I've taken pains to acknowledge the obstacles people face so as not to create a romantic or unrealistic account of citizen politics. Now, in this chapter, I want to say more about the age-old argument that most people aren't able to meet the demands of democratic citizenship. These arguments are still around; they can't be easily dismissed. And maybe they shouldn't be. I'll also compare what critics say about the citizenry with what people say about the criticism.

> *The average American doesn't want to be educated;*
> *he doesn't want to improve his mind; he doesn't even*
> *want to work, consciously, at being a good citizen.*
>
> —Clem Whitaker[1]

NOT REALLY! AND THEY SHOULDN'T!

The quotation in this chapter's title is from Alexander Hamilton, who actually had serious reservations about people's ability to rule themselves. He would have limited that rule to governing indirectly through electing representatives in the lower house of legislative bodies.[2] Although many Americans believe they should rule—and without the limitation of just electing representatives, which Hamilton favored— they meet resistance on multiple fronts and struggle to respond to critics and skeptics. These reservations about citizens go back to Plato's era and probably much earlier. In America, prominent journalist Walter Lippmann argued that the supposedly sovereign public is no more than a phantom of our political imagination.[3] His argument lives on.

Here, sir, the people govern; here they act by their immediate representatives.

—Alexander Hamilton

A college textbook charges that the majority of Americans are apathetic about politics—that people just don't care:

> Democracy is government "by the people," but the responsibility for the survival of democracy rests on the shoulders of elites. This is the irony of democracy: Elites must govern wisely if government "by the people" is to survive. If the survival of the U.S. system depended on an active, informed, and enlightened citizenry, then democracy in the United States would have disappeared long ago, for the many are apathetic and ill-informed about politics and public policy, and they exhibit a surprisingly weak commitment to democratic values. . . . Fortunately for these values and for U.S. democracy, the masses do not lead; they follow.[4]

This criticism isn't confined to textbooks. A significant number of leaders, national and local, have the same opinion of citizens. As one of them said bluntly about his community, "Democracy just doesn't work here."

In this same vein, John Hibbing and Elizabeth Theiss-Morse report in *Stealth Democracy* that few people have strong feelings on most issues and prefer to have their representatives make those decisions. They aren't willing to be a Ruth, Gene, Sandy, Max, or Sue.[5] On the other hand, other political scientists strenuously object to such conclusions. These scholars have amassed considerable evidence that what appears to be public indifference is actually not that at all but rather a reaction to a dysfunctional political system.[6]

This contrary evidence notwithstanding, maybe a democracy should remain open to its challenges. Rather than trying to refute charges that citizens aren't up to the demands of self-rule, it might be better to try to engage the critics by recognizing the validity of some of their observations about lapses of good citizenship, which frustrate even public-minded folk like Ruth and Gene.

PUBLIC PARTICIPATION AND OFFICEHOLDERS' FRUSTRATION

Despite (or perhaps because of) being involved in failed attempts at getting the public involved, local and federal officeholders (as well as those in civic organizations) have produced long lists of frustrations. They say that most people don't respond when asked to become involved; consequently, corporate and other special interests dominate politics. They believe citizens distrust one another and disagree (particularly by race and class). They don't find many situations where people are working together. If citizens do become interested in an issue, so the complaints go, they are usually just emotionally involved and make ill-advised decisions. For example, people are said to favor

Source: CartoonStock.com

cutting taxes without cutting government benefits. Officials are especially frustrated when people don't trust them or their institutions.

Other critics say there really isn't much people can do politically;
they don't have the resources and are too disorganized to be effective;
everyone wants to go his or her own way. Citizen volunteers are frequently unreliable and irresponsible. And there isn't any way to compel
them to do what they've promised. Even when a project gets started,
it often stops short of its goal; the momentum is easily lost. There also
isn't any way to tell whether civic efforts have been effective; citizens
seldom evaluate, at least not objectively.

Even if none of these criticisms are valid, building civic capacity in
a community takes years, realists argue, and the effort doesn't produce
the hard numbers that funders or government programs demand.

Given these unhappy experiences with citizens, no wonder leaders
at every level have serious reservations about involving them. Taking
issues to the public or, worse, relying on people's decisions strikes some
as either naïve or downright dangerous. Others feel overwhelmed at
the thought of airing issues in the community because they believe it
only gives more power to the most vocal.[7]

Officials heading large institutions also fault citizens for being
hopelessly parochial in a global society. They don't see the connection
that the Harwood research found between people solving local problems and national well-being.[8] When people do get involved, these
critics say, it is always on a problem close to home. Yet in more and
more situations, they argue, the solutions to problems have come from
larger regions—a metro area or a group of neighboring counties. Citizens may agree with the need for a regional response, yet sometimes,
the "region" they have in mind goes no more than 15 miles from their
front door.

Other evidence of parochialism: in *The Big Sort*, Bill Bishop argues
that people are increasingly moving into like-minded enclaves, which
undermines their ability to work together on a larger scale. "Finding
cultural comfort in 'people like us,'" Bishop believes, "we have migrated

"Things have gotten bad here. There's talk of a war with another gated community."

into ever-narrower communities and churches and political groups . . . distinguished by their isolation and single-mindedness."[9]

FROM THE PUBLIC'S POINT OF VIEW

I have no reason to doubt that leaders, representatives, and officials have had the disappointments they say they have. On the other hand, people's perception that they have been pushed out of the political system seems quite valid. Certainly, declining confidence in institutions is real, and much of it seems to be based on the feeling that schools, government agencies, and large nongovernmental organizations aren't responsive.

A study by John Creighton found that the public's perception of all leaders has grown darker. He reports, "[P]oliticians—along with corporate executives, Wall Street bankers, and the wealthy in general—are [seen as] immune from and . . . indifferent to the hardships of ordinary Americans." Money per se didn't seem as much a problem, however, as greed and a lack of regard for others. Citizens in this study reasoned that new rules to curb the influence of money wouldn't help as long as "the political class is committed to circumventing any reform."[10] The political system seems intractable, and some citizens have become intransigent in response. They've become even more determined to throw tea into harbors or sit in at the citadels of power. Others, unable to trust institutional leaders, feel that their only alternative is to look to themselves and those they know well enough to count on.[11] (This response may account for what some see as parochialism.)

The public's lack of trust in leaders and institutions has been around for decades; it isn't some passing mood. Research in the 1990s showed Americans fuming about being pushed out of their rightful place in governing the nation.[12] They were convinced that votes seldom made a difference in a system with its doors closed to the average citizen. The research went beneath the usual popular dissatisfaction with government and politicians to discover not only strong feelings about powerlessness and exclusion, but also an untapped sense of civic duty. According to the study, no interpretation of the public is less accurate than the often-repeated contention that people are too consumed with private matters to care about politics. Those who participated in the study had a clear sense of their civic responsibilities. They cared so deeply that their frustration ran to anger and cynicism—a cynicism they worried about passing on to their children.[13]

People talked about being shut out of institutional politics as they would if they had come home one evening to find the house locked and someone else inside wearing their clothes and eating their food. And they knew who had locked them out. They pointed their fingers at incumbent politicians, campaign managers, powerful lobbyists, and those in the media. They saw these groups as a professional political class, the rulers of an oligarchy that had replaced democracy. Politics was a game for the "big guns," particularly special interest groups. Citizens were relegated to the margins of the political system, where they

stood unable to influence either the players or the rules of the game.[14] These perceptions and feelings that were evident in the 1990s are still with us.

STRUCTURAL CHANGES: CITIZEN-LITE DEMOCRACY

As you can see, some research shows that most Americans have a strong sense of civic duty and are active in the politics they won't call politics; other reports argue that people are apathetic or retreating from civic life into narrow enclaves of the like minded. The evidence appears contradictory, but one trend is well documented: whether or not people are disposed to be involved, the avenues they have traditionally used to get into politics have been closing.

Two scholars, Matthew Crenson and Benjamin Ginsberg, have documented this long-term trend to sideline citizens and privatize public life. They describe numerous ways that have been devised to make a collective citizenry unnecessary:

> Political elites have found ways to achieve their policy objectives without mobilizing voters. Rather than take issues to the electorate for resolution, today's contending elites attempt to outdo their opponents by litigating, [or] by manipulating administrative procedures . . . that remove policy to arenas beyond the reach of their rivals. In the process, the millions of citizens who might once have been called to the aid of their parties now remain passive bystanders. Yesterday's actors have become today's audience—spectators and customers rather than citizens.[15]

At best, Crenson and Ginsberg note, citizens are treated as customers to be served. Their role is to choose, much as consumers would, from shelves of political leaders, policies, and government programs. This privatizes citizens in a personal sort of democracy, leaving no place for people to exercise their collective power in the interest of the polity as a whole. Power comes instead from the many "publics" that are formed around particular, rather than inclusive, interests. The role of governments is to bargain or negotiate with these interest groups.

Citizens have also been sidelined because the organizations that were once vehicles for civic action have changed. As Theda Skocpol's research shows, "there are too few opportunities for large numbers of Americans to work together for broadly shared values and interests." That has happened as the number of special interest groups lobbying in Washington and state capitols has mushroomed. Between 1960 and 1990, the number of national associations, including public interest groups, Skocpol reports, increased from 6,000 to 23,000.[16]

During this same time period, many of the civic groups also changed in character. No longer membership associations, they moved to Washington to be lobbyists; or they adopted new forms of organizations as staff-centered think tanks and political action committees.

Mass membership became less important than a large war chest. So members turned into donors, substituting money for their civic work. Volunteer leadership, in turn, gave way to professional staffs that organized media campaigns to influence legislation—usually on very specific issues. These changes may have been beneficial to the organizations, yet the costs to self-rule were significant. The declining membership organizations were not available to bridge class barriers and to champion broad-based, inclusive social programs.[17]

> *America's civic life has shifted from membership*
> *mobilization to advocacy and management and from*
> *stress on shared values and goals to the pursuit of*
> *specialized interests.*
>
> —Theda Skocpol[18]

People not only feel that their ownership of public institutions has declined but also doubt that the situation will ever improve. People fear that our major institutions can't be reformed or reform themselves.

On the positive side of the ledger, between 1960 and 1990, minorities and women entered the mainstream, making the political system more representative of the population. That has been good for self-rule. Yet at the same time, more power shifted to the unelected branches, the bureaucracies and courts. Furthermore, the citadel of citizen power, the local community, has lost standing as a consideration in policy-making.[19] The "place of place," as Martha Derthick put it, referring to geographic communities, has been diminished.

Americans don't just feel estranged from institutions; some have misgivings as well about the citizens who aren't their family and friends. They aren't sure that they can count on these "strangers" to support them. So, despite exemplary cases of collective efforts by citizens to improve the well-being of all, and despite an awareness of civic duties and social responsibilities, the citizenry has sometimes sidelined itself out of uncertainty, except perhaps when there is a crisis that brings people together for a while.[20] Though a bit ashamed of retreating into enclaves, many don't see any alternative because of their doubts about other people.

> *The experience of democracy is like the experience of life itself—always changing, infinite in its variety, sometimes turbulent and all the more valuable for having been tested by adversity.*
>
> —Jimmy Carter[21]

5
PUTTING THE PUBLIC BACK
IN THE PUBLIC'S BUSINESS

ALTHOUGH AWARE OF THE CRITICISMS directed at citizens, having doubts about strategies, and hearing pronouncements about democracy not working, a great many Americans refuse to sit quietly on the sidelines. And they have reasons for their determination.

THE CASE FOR CITIZENSHIP

Arguments for getting citizens off the sidelines fall into two categories. One consists of claims about citizens' sovereignty under the Bill of Rights and Constitution. The other category is made up of practical considerations about the work of citizens that is required to combat problems that bedevil communities and plague institutions. The two lines of argument actually converge into one, which is that it takes the power in civic work to make the constitutional power in the ballot box meaningful.

The Logic of Public Sovereignty

Elliot Richardson, whose extraordinary career was in government (most notably in four Cabinet positions in Washington), once said: "Although we the people have delegated limited responsibilities to those who hold public office in the interest of all of us, we, nevertheless, retain ultimate responsibility. We cannot delegate it; it belongs to us. We may fulfill it well or poorly, but still we have it."[1] Some might interpret these nondelegable responsibilities as a mandate for endless referenda dictating what government should do.[2] Citizens would be voters to be consulted, to give their consent and to be represented. But these roles connect citizens to the state or government; they say nothing about citizenship as defined by people's political relations to one another. And that is where the nondelegable responsibilities begin.

A country as large and diverse as the United States has to have representative government. Still, electing representatives isn't all there is to the sovereignty that the Constitution places in the citizenry. If people believe they are sovereign with nondelegable responsibilities, what else does that mean?

I believe that the only way for sovereign power to be real, not abstract, is for people to exercise their sovereignty through their civic work. As I've said, the work that citizens do with citizens—and the things that work produces—these give citizens the power they need to be true sovereigns.

> *The health of a democratic society may be measured by*
> *the quality of functions performed by private citizens.*
>
> —Attributed to Alexis de Tocqueville[3]

Here is the logic behind this assumption about civic work and sovereignty: monarchs exercise power by acting. A king or queen wouldn't be a sovereign for very long without the power to act. That is the reason a sovereign citizenry must be a political actor, a producer, not just a beneficiary or constituency. A democratic public can't be a dependent body to be acted for or upon. It has to be able to act, producing things that benefit all.

The things civic work produces have been called "public goods"— goods that are made by the public for the public. Historically, the things citizens have made have included schools, hospitals—even the country itself. Today, the products of citizens' collective efforts—their civic work—include the neighborhood gardens that Ernesto described.[4]

A Different Kind of Activism: Capacity Building

The case for citizen sovereignty is being made today, not by arguments, but by action. Citizens have long been advocates of worthwhile causes or organizers solving specific problems and carrying out particular projects. Now we are seeing another group of citizens emerging who have a broader focus, often the well-being of a community as a whole, not just a specific cause or project. These activists aim at increasing the civic capacity of their community, the capacity for solving problems and becoming more resilient when faced with challenges. Kettering first became acquainted with these kinds of citizens when sponsors of deliberative town meetings used the National Issues Forums to build a greater local capacity for shared decision making on contentious issues. (The citizens who started the Grand Rapids forums are examples.)

A study by Harvard faculty described these capacity builders as "entrepreneurs" rather than advocates, and the name stuck.[5] These citizens (Sue comes to mind) like having such a distinctive title, and they deserve it because they usually start from nowhere with no one to support them. Like political environmentalists, they often use local resources. They also see themselves and their roles as different from community leaders or organizers. They see their job as being spark plugs to encourage innovation and strengthen the capacity for self-rule. Not wedded to a particular cause, they concentrate on improving neighborhoods or their town as a whole. As capacity builders, they focus on strengthening the ways citizens have of solving common problems.

The Harvard study found that these capacity-building entrepreneurs are especially adept at forming alliances as well as locating opportunities to introduce new ways of collective decision making and acting. They are risk takers who aren't looking so much for safe havens as opportunities to make a difference. They experiment. As might be expected, these citizens typically operate outside of or at the borders of existing organizations—or they create their own associations. They work on building pragmatic relations with other citizens, which is a form of capacity building.

This brand of civic activism didn't come out of nowhere. Creating pragmatic "public" relationships has long been a hallmark of the work of community organizers like Gerald Taylor of the Industrial Areas Foundation (IAF). For Taylor, building public relationships begins with acknowledging differences among interests rather than trying to homogenize them. The objective of creating these relationships is to promote cooperation, even when interests differ, because interests are often related. That is to say, different interests are often interdependent and can be connected.

A story in the archives of IAF describes how pragmatic relationships are created: When leaders of Baltimore BUILD, a local civic organization, first met with Senator Paul Sarbanes, he smiled, took out his notebook, and asked what he could do for them. The leaders said, in effect, "Nothing, we're here to get to know you. We want to know why you're in the U.S. Senate and what your interests are. Your inter-

Illustration by Jennifer Berman

We may have all come on different ships,
but we're in the same boat now.

— Attributed to Martin Luther King Jr.[7]

ests may be connected to some of ours. If they are, we may be able to develop a working relationship over time."[6]

The objective of building pragmatic relationships is to change the way people habitually deal with one another—to get beyond conflict and lack of trust. These relationships are formed around self-interests, which will differ. The goal isn't to get people to agree or like and understand one another. Just getting folks to talk together may be a big accomplishment, but people soon get impatient with just talk; they want problems to be solved. And that's a call for pragmatism.

Nearly all capacity builders report being pressed for immediate solutions to what they know are problems that can't be eliminated quickly or easily. As one of them told me, those who think there are both short-term and long-term approaches to fundamental problems are mistaken. There aren't any short-term solutions, she said, only long-term ones.

As is true of most activists, capacity builders occasionally harbor ambivalent feelings about their fellow citizens. For instance, they fear that people will stop work on a project that they have helped launch if they aren't always present to encourage or prod. At the same time, they are sensitive to creating dependence if they are constantly on hand. These obstacles notwithstanding, capacity builders are a persistent lot. They usually bounce back from disappointments and press on. Since they draw on the local resources in their communities, they are able to keep going. Their first response to a challenge isn't, "Where can we get the money?" Though not averse to greenbacks, they know there are other currencies—time, goodwill, networks, and the other wetland resources.[8]

Sovereignty in the Making

Joining forces to do civic work typically begins quite ordinarily.[9] On any given day, someone takes the first step to becoming involved by talking to family and friends about an incident that bothers them. Then they might try to find out whether anyone outside this close circle is also worried. For instance, a woman might talk with her neighbors about drug paraphernalia she saw in the street.[10] It could be a short conversation, probably over her backyard fence. At the next stage, conversations become more structured when they are carried into churches and civic organizations. Later still, town meetings might be held on what should be done to keep drugs out of the community, and people might decide on a strategy. Some of the things they decide to do could be carried out by ad hoc groups or civic associations. Government agencies would most likely be asked to play a role as well.

Participation usually begins on a very personal level. Americans worry about *their* jobs, *their* health, *their* children's education. And they keep coming back to these primary concerns, which remain political touchstones. When people are asked to consider an issue, the first thing they usually ask themselves is, "Does this problem affect me or my family?" They focus on what is most valuable.

Returning to the example of someone discovering drug paraphernalia, when people try to find out if anyone else shares their concerns, they begin to have conversations in the places where people routinely gather. They move in and out of a great many discussions, most of which are random and unstructured. Much of what they say may sound like small talk—with a lot of personal stories thrown in. People are just mulling over what they hear or perhaps testing for a response: What did you see? What do you think it means? It worries me, does it worry you? At this point, they aren't ready to make decisions; they are still checking out the situation, and that takes time.

As people gather more and more information, it might seem that they would become confused, that a deluge of facts and opinions would overwhelm them, but this isn't necessarily the case. While citizens can certainly be overwhelmed, they usually try to make connections among related problems. They experience the combined effects of interrelated problems in their everyday lives, so they try to find out how the different pieces fit together. For example, when drug abuse soars, people look for the sources of the problem in everything from the stability of family life to the condition of the economy. They don't simplify issues; they try to see how they are interrelated.[11]

When people realize that they share similar concerns, they tend to feel connected to one another; they don't have to see the same problem in the same way, however. In fact, people seldom do because their circumstances and experiences aren't the same. Yet if citizens realize they all have a stake in solving a problem, albeit for different reasons, they are disposed to form alliances. As IAF found, people can realize that, although their interests are different, they are interdependent. On the other hand, when people fail to see these interrelations or to make these connections, they feel isolated and unable to make a difference.

A Thousand People Spurring Another Thousand

Why are we seeing more capacity builders? Why—given the doubts about democracy and citizens—do many Americans persist in thinking citizens should, indeed, govern themselves? History helps answer the question.

Robert Wiebe tells the story of how citizen politics came to define democracy in frontier America, despite the ruling elite's preference for a republic and not a democracy. Wiebe writes, "The driving force behind 19th century democracy was thousands of people spurring thousands of other people to act."[12] Wiebe had voting in mind, but I think his observation is accurate when applied to civic efforts. The democracy of self-rule was rooted in shared decision making and acting—especially acting. Settlers on the frontier had no choice but to be producers, not just consumers. They had to join forces to build forts, roads, and libraries. They formed associations to combat alcoholism and care for the poor. They established the first public schools.[13]

The habit of collective enterprise is still with us. More recently, citizen-initiated movements have sprung up to protect the environment and secure rights for minorities. This collective effort occurs in an American culture that also promotes individual responsibility and self-sufficiency. Perhaps individual responsibility and civic responsibility are two sides of the same coin.

> Citizens joined together in civic work makes the democratic
> public more than an aggregation of individuals. This public
> is not a mass of people, nor is it the public of surveys and
> polls based on individuals expressing their own personal
> opinions without the benefit of hearing the views of other
> citizens. What is public is also more than what is popular.[14]

WHAT ONLY A CITIZENRY CAN DO

In laying out the reasons for putting the public back in the public's
business, I don't want to neglect the role citizens play in promoting
democratic rights. Maybe the greatest incentive for a citizen-centered
democracy is that many people want to lead a democratic life because
they cherish liberty and the pursuit of public happiness (the fulfillment
that comes from having a civic life). Never perfectly achieved, democracy is a journey to realize these rights, however elusive.

That said, the subject now is not the citizenry's role in protecting democratic rights but rather practical reasons for not sidelining
citizens. I would call back to "the witness stand" Elinor Ostrom, who
pointed out that neither communities nor institutions can do their
work effectively without support from the work of citizens.[15] That is
because many of our most difficult problems can't be solved without
the goods produced by citizens. Even our largest and most powerful institutions need this reinforcement because they face problems
so "wicked" that they defy our best professionals and most powerful
agencies.

Combating the Wickedness in Problems

These most difficult problems have been called "wicked" as compared
to "tamer" problems that have technical solutions.[16] An example: hard-
core poverty that persists in the face of prosperity.

Wicked problems have several defining characteristics. One is that people disagree on what should be done about them, and the disagreements are moral or ethical. People are troubled by discrepancies between what is happening to them and what they think *should be* happening—yet don't agree on what the problems are, much less what *should* be done about them. Since the disputes aren't over questions of fact but over what is the *right* thing to do, citizens have to judge for themselves. The ability of citizens to exercise sound judgment in the face of disagreements and uncertainty is critical. There aren't any experts on what is right.

Source: CartoonStock.com

"We've finally addressed the problem. Now find a stamp and get it outta here!"

Another defining characteristic of wicked problems is that the citizenry has to respond. People have to act because they have resources that are different from those of institutions. These are wetland resources that include personal skills and experiences as well as collective caring and the ability to form pragmatic work relationships. The wetlands also generate the civic energy needed to deploy such resources.[17] In a word, citizens have to work together in order to combat truly wicked problems.

Wicked problems are not only more human than technical, but also so deeply embedded in the social fabric that they never completely go away. They are as tricky as they are aggressive. Each symptom exposes another problem in a never-ending chain. Coping with these problems requires sustained civic action that doesn't begin at one point and end at another, but, instead, continues in a series of richly diverse initiatives.

Sustained action also has to be comprehensive because wicked problems have multiple sources found in every sector of a community. Communities as a whole have to respond. One group or one section of a town won't be effective.

Actually, most all public problems have a degree of wickedness in them; that is, they are all subject to morally charged disagreements. Differences in what people hold dear give rise to different options for action: "The right thing to do is take care of children first." "No, we should be taking care of the elderly because of all the hard work they have done for us."

Even within a given option, there can be tensions over what is most valuable. Should we give aid directly to children or create more prekindergarten programs? Every course of action has disadvantages as well as advantages. Gaining something of value often requires compromising something else of value. I'll say more about this later, but most decisions force us to make very difficult choices. The work citizens need to do together begins in making these hard choices.

Avoiding Solution Wars

The problems of democracy are usually behind the wicked problems in our democracy. And wicked problems can't be addressed without dealing with the more basic problems of democracy itself. Since most people don't want to just talk about wicked problems but to do something about them, they have to confront the malfunctions of democracy that impair self-rule. For example, not recognizing and working through the morally charged disagreements characteristic of wicked problems can lock communities into never-ending, unproductive "solution wars." These conflicts arise when pressure to find the "right solution" draws a community into a battle among proponents of competing plans. Communities have been known to waste energy debating which of a number of predetermined solutions is best when there has been little attention given to the nature of the problem or the resources needed to combat it.

The problems in health care are a case in point because resources that only citizens can contribute are invaluable. Institutions can care *for* people but not *about* them in the way that people do. In addition to family and friends, larger "networks of nurture" organized by communities can be a potent force in combating the behavioral and social problems that contribute to many illnesses.[18] This has been demonstrated in research done for the Centers for Disease Control and Prevention, which shows that community care can reduce the incidence of heart disease, strokes, and lung cancer.[19]

Complementary Production Makes Sense

Citizens can't be left on the sidelines, not only because they are indispensible in recognizing and combating wicked problems, but also because their work is needed to complement the work of governments, schools, and other institutions. This was Elinor Ostrom's very practical argument for a citizen-centered democracy:

> If one presumes that teachers produce education, police produce safety, doctors and nurses produce health, and social workers produce effective households, the focus of attention is on how to professionalize the public service. Obviously, skilled teachers, police officers, medical personnel, and social workers are essential to the development of better public services. Ignoring the important role of children, families, support groups, neighborhood organizations, and churches in the production

of these services means, however, that only a portion of the inputs to these processes are taken into account in the way that policy makers think about these problems. The term "client" is used more and more frequently to refer to those who should be viewed as essential co-producers of their own education, safety, health, and communities. A client is the name for a passive role. Being a co-producer makes one an active partner.[20]

Products from the work of citizens can complement what institutions do because civic work is different from the work of institutions. I am not talking about such things as volunteering to take the load off teachers and health care professionals, although that is very commendable. I have in mind supplementary projects that involve people doing the things professionals don't—and can't—do. That's why I use the term "complementary production" rather than "coproduction." A simple example: citizens organizing themselves to walk children through dangerous neighborhoods on the way to school. That is not what professionals are trained to do (even though teachers are often called on to do guard duty).

Another example: The work of schools is teaching, which is part, but not all, of educating. Schools can benefit enormously from what citizens do with citizens to prepare the next generation of young people for the future. While most formal instruction is best left to professionals, people believe they can educate. And what children learn in educating institutions other than schools can reinforce what happens in classrooms. These institutions, which are in and of the community, provide a valuable real world context for learning. In Kentucky, a farm for retired racehorses has been used to supplement classroom instruction.[21] And there has been complementary production in Alabama where contextual learning is being promoted by an organization called PACERS, a cooperative association of rural schools.[22] PACERS has used things citizens have built (solar homes, greenhouses, fishponds as well as local newsrooms) as learning laboratories. These efforts have had a positive impact on classroom performance. There are similar cases in other states. The citizens who organize these initiatives pull the community together around a project and then bring the young people into it as a means of enriching their education.[23] This is community organizing with a twist—the objective is to use the resources of the community to educate.

In Lexington, Kentucky, Bruce Mundy, who understood wetland resources, and a group of adults worried about kids who came to his afterschool program. He said, "I've got kids who can't read. To me, that is a crisis." Bruce got kids to start hacking away at the ten-foot weeds around an old cemetery, which proved to be an invaluable resource. The youngsters found the gravesites of African American Civil War veterans and winning jockeys in the Kentucky Derby. The students researched those names and got the (now pristine) site on the National Register of Historic Places. "'Scuse me while I teach history!" Bruce joked. He believes that, like the backward-looking Sankofa bird, kids need to know where they come from to find where they're going. Youngsters painted trashcans to share the history they had learned. Whatever they had, they used, like creating sculptures from junk bicycles. It's interesting that Bruce did all this while serving as an employee of the health department.[24] He and his friends' efforts complete what schools and other educating institutions do.

The more people talk about education, the more they turn their attention to their communities and to educating institutions other than schools. No one illustrates that better than a Baton Rouge resident who reasoned there should be "a community strategy, not a school strategy, for educating every single child."[25]

WHAT'S AT STAKE

The work of citizens in these examples defines a particular kind of democracy, which I would say is citizen-rich. This understanding of democracy is crucial because of what it adds to a worldwide contest over the meaning of this form of government. The contest is real. Americans have witnessed it in Tea Party rallies and in Occupy Wall Street protests. And the world has seen the contest in the revolutions of the Arab Spring. Given these upheavals and the not-too-distant memories of velvet (and not so velvet) revolutions in Europe and elsewhere in the 1980s and 1990s, it is crucial to make the work of citizens visible in this contest.

This contest is not a battle among competing ideologies like communism and capitalism or between representative and direct democracy. Rather, it is a contest deep within democracy itself, and the outcome will ultimately be decided by the citizens, not authorities of any sort. The key issue is what role citizens see for themselves. That won't be determined in abstract debates but issue by issue as people decide what they are or aren't willing to do as citizens. Democracy isn't going to fade away, yet the form that survives may be "citizen lite," that is, a democracy with citizens and civic work on the margins.

There have always been differing viewpoints on the applied meaning of democracy. Which is right? Since the people are the supreme authority, there is no power over them that can say, once and for all, what democracy means. "We the people" have to decide that, community by community, country by country, and decade by decade. The question of what kind of democracy we will have *in* the future boils down to how much responsibility people are willing to take *for* the future.

6
CITIZENS: INVOLVED AND INFORMED?

I BELIEVE THAT AMERICA NEEDS the work citizens do with citizens in order to deal with persistent, truly wicked problems and to complement the efforts of schools, governments, and other institutions. But there are serious problems of democracy itself that stand in the way of getting this work done.

Two problems of democracy stand out. People are too often on the sidelines of the political system. Furthermore, simply being involved won't result in a better life for all unless citizens make informed and wise decisions about what should be done. So what motivates people to get involved, and what gives them the ability to make sound decisions?

WHY GET INVOLVED?

Many of us become involved with other citizens because we are trying to solve a problem or influence an elected body or major institution. We may be supercharged by a cause we care about, or we are directly affected by something that is about to happen or needs to happen: "We can't let our school close!" Most people, however, aren't zealots and aren't directly affected by every political decision. Still, all of us are motivated by deeply held concerns about the future and what is at stake for us.

Our most basic political motives—the things that move us to engage with others outside our circle of family and friends—may spring from the lessons our ancestors learned about survival. There is now enough archaeological and biological (DNA) research to make some reasonable assumptions about these prehistoric times. Our earliest forebearers, who survived by hunting and gathering food, likely valued their freedom to forage and look for game. It is also reasonable to think they valued the security that comes from joining forces, which was essential in tasks like hunting. And they may have come to appreciate fairness because the bands they lived in wouldn't stay together unless the benefits from their collective efforts were distributed equitably. Simply put, those who participated in a hunting expedition would want a place in the feast that followed. Given these formative influences, we humans may be programmed to prize freedom, collective security, and equity.

Early humans were also no strangers to violent conflict. Yet it is not farfetched to assume that our ancestors would have valued the things that kept them secure from danger and helped them prosper.[1] But

"O.K., we get it—big and dangerous."

Source: Robert Leighton, The New Yorker Collection, cartoonbank.com

regardless of whether these conjectures about our early ancestors are right, when making difficult decisions today, people will often call to mind the things that are fundamental to their well-being.

I've found that if I use the word *values* to describe these primary motivations, people naturally think I am talking about "VALUES." Hodding Carter Jr. told me that he thought of values as "the parts of the Bible printed in red ink." That's not what I am talking about. I am referring to the most essential things that people hold dear. Today, social psychologists recognize these as the ends or purposes of life and the means necessary to reaching those ends.[2]

What is deeply valuable collectively or politically is different from the interests that grow out of our particular circumstances as well as distinct from abstract values or our personal beliefs. Political imperatives are similar to the individual imperatives psychologist Abraham Maslow found common to all human beings, like food, water, and shelter.

I want to emphasize that the things critically important to our collective well-being are common to most everyone. Most of us want to be secure from danger. We want to be free to advance our own well-being. We want to be treated fairly by others. These imperatives motivate us to become politically active. They are passions deep in our souls.

Some of the things individuals require are quite tangible (food, for instance), while others (being loved) are less so. The same is true in collective matters. I learned that from a community that was facing corruption in high places and egregious crimes in the streets. Citizens there asked themselves what they valued most. Nearly all said that, more than anything, they wanted to live in a place that made them proud. Pride is a source of identity, a necessity since ancient times. But this intangible aspiration is rarely mentioned in planning documents or lists of goals. Still, the need to be proud of a city can be a powerful political incentive.

The importance of taking into consideration the things people value is illustrated in Wendell Berry's story of an agricultural economist who told farmers that there was little difference between renting and owning land. One farmer responded by telling the economist that his forebearers didn't come to America to be renters.[3] Something the farmer valued in addition to profits was at stake: it was the security of land ownership. My grandfather, who farmed, said of land, "They aren't making any more of it, you know."

What's in a Name?

Americans who appear to be uninterested in politics may simply fail to see much connection between what they consider valuable and the policy issues championed by interest groups, pressed by community leaders, debated by politicians, and discussed in the media. The names professionals give issues may be technically precise yet often fail to resonate with the things people hold dear. Getting people off the sidelines may be less a matter of arousing the indifferent than making connections with the things people already care about.

Nearly every day something—perhaps surprising, often troubling—happens. Test scores show a significant gap in the academic performance of different groups of students. The United States spends more on health care per capita than other countries, but the results aren't as good. When faced with these problems, people begin to talk about what they read or hear. What's the problem? Soon, newspapers, TV shows, and Internet blogs come out with explanations. Politicians begin to make pronouncements about what is going on; they give the problem a name like the "achievement gap" and explain what they think should be done.

The name given to a problem may seem a trifling matter, yet in politics, it isn't. Who gets to name a problem, and the name itself, have everything to do with who gets involved in solving it. It turns out that naming holds a key to countering a serious problem of democracy—people not becoming involved as citizens. For example, the "achievement gap" is a label used by politicians and educators, but it doesn't always resonate with people. They see the academic gap as a symptom of many other gaps, such as economic ones.[4]

SOUND JUDGMENT OR HASTY DECISIONS?

Becoming involved is only half the battle. Once involved, people may act together, but it's no blessing unless they act wisely so society as a whole benefits. Critics worry that the public's participation won't be well informed. And much of the institutional and professional hesitation to involve the public comes from worries that citizens won't make thoughtful decisions.

A woman whose home was surrounded by rental properties saw a fistfight break out in front of one of them. Based on that one incident, which alarmed her, she decided that the problem was one of loose codes for rental homes. Without the benefit of other information, such as actual crime rates or police reports, she built a huge grassroots movement using e-mail and social media. She and her followers started putting pressure on the city government. A new, very strict rental ordinance was passed that made life more difficult for law-abiding renters. Fear reached an emotional level that didn't allow for thoughtful decision making.[5]

As in this case, being informed politically involves having facts, but facts alone aren't sufficient. People have to exercise sound judgment on issues that are morally charged and can't be resolved with facts alone. These are situations where the issue is what is "right." The usual response in such situations is to "educate" the people by giving them the correct information—certainly nothing wrong with that. Yet no amount of information is enough to fully inform the kind of decisions citizens have to make when the question is about the *right* thing to do. Should schools provide more courses in math and science, even if that means reducing those in the humanities and dropping physical education? Should we put stricter controls on the Internet, even if that would infringe on free speech? These questions can be answered in more than one way and require the exercise of judgment. The things people hold dear or consider deeply valuable are at stake and have to be considered, which is why informing our decisions requires more than facts alone.

"My problem is that I am an informed citizen."

Here's an example of the difference between questions of fact and questions of judgment: How long a bridge must be in order to span a river and how strong it must be to bear the weight of traffic are factual questions. But whether we should build a bridge in fragile coastal wetlands is more than a question of fact. Although facts are certainly relevant, deciding to build a bridge to a barrier island requires the exercise of our best judgment about the right thing to do—given all that we consider valuable.

Questions of judgment are especially difficult to answer because we hold a great many things dear. We have to weigh our options carefully against the various imperatives that tug at us. We do that when making individual decisions in everyday life.

Imagine someone coming home from a hard day at work and looking forward to quiet and rest. But his or her spouse, who has been taking care of the home and family, wants to get out of the house and go to a new restaurant for dinner. The children, however, want to go to a movie. Then, before those conflicts can be resolved, in-laws call, complain of being neglected, and insist the family spend the evening at their house. The spouse, the children, and even the in-laws are *all* important. Giving one priority over another usually isn't a good idea. And the must-see movie begins soon, so the parents have to make a decision quickly; there isn't time to negotiate with all the parties involved.

After weighing the pros and cons of possible options, the couple decides to go to dinner and drop the kids off at the movie theater on the way. They postpone the evening with the in-laws to later in the week. They make some trade-offs and balance demands or competing imperatives as best they can. We do much the same thing when making decisions with other citizens.

Making decisions with those who are not family or friends is challenging because what people value has different meanings for different people. That's because we live in different circumstances. I value security, and because I live in a neighborhood where there are a lot of break-ins, I want a visible police presence. My friend, who also values security, lives in a safe neighborhood and doesn't want it turned into an armed camp. Just because people value the same things doesn't mean they agree.

The Human Faculty for Judgment

When making a decision about what is right and people disagree, we have to rely on our faculty for judgment. Briefly defined, a judgment is said to be sound if it is consistent with what we consider most valuable in a particular situation. Driving slowly on a wet highway is a sound decision because it makes us safer, even though we may be late for a meeting. Because we value many things—our security from danger, our freedom to act, and so on—we have to determine, given the circumstances facing us, which is most valuable or, failing in that, how best to balance competing imperatives.

The neurosciences help explain how the human faculty for judgment works.[6] Studies have shown that an exchange of experiences with others, exposure to a diversity of opinions, and consideration of all alternatives create the ideal situation for good decisions.[7] These conditions are found in deliberative practice, which I'll say more about in the next chapter.

Of course, people don't always make sound decisions. Just because we have a faculty for judgment doesn't mean we always use it. Public decision making is difficult, sometimes bruising, and there are thousands of ways of avoiding it in a culture that promotes sound bites and partisan debate. All that is natural isn't easy, and it can even be rare.

Having a faculty for judgment, I should add, doesn't mean that the citizenry has a corner on a special wisdom that officeholders, institutional leaders, and professionals don't have—or if they did they wouldn't make so many dumb mistakes. Furthermore, even if people's conclusions are consistent with what they value, there aren't any guarantees that their decision will prove to be the best one. We have no way of knowing what a decision will produce until its effects have played out over time.

Illustration by Jennifer Berman

There must be discussion and debate, in which all freely
participate. . . . The whole purpose of democracy is that we
may hold counsel with another. . . . For only [then] . . .
can the general interests of a great people be compounded
into a policy that will be suitable to all.

—Woodrow Wilson[8]

7
PUBLIC DELIBERATION AND PUBLIC JUDGMENT

ANCIENT LANGUAGES HAVE LEFT US A CLUE as to how we can make use of our faculty for judgment. It is the word *deliberation*, which is found in different written forms, from Egyptian hieroglyphics to old Chinese characters. To deliberate is to carefully weigh possible civic actions, laws, or policies against the various things that people hold dear in order to settle on a direction to follow or purpose to pursue.

DELIBERATING TO DECIDE

Deliberation or, more precisely, public deliberation is an apt term because of its history. I'll digress a bit into that history because it helps clarify what it takes for the public to inform itself. In Latin, the "libera" in *deliberation* refers to a scale (*libra*) used to weigh (*librare*) in order to determine worth. In situations when there are competing imperatives about what is worth most to us and our collective well-being, we deliberate with others to make decisions.

Weighing (as on a scale) in the process of determining the worth of something exercises our faculty for judgment. And judgment informs our decisions, making them sound. Personally, I like Pericles' concept of deliberation as the talk (*logo*) used before people act in order to

Illustration by Jennifer Berman

first teach themselves (*prodidacthenai*) how to act.[1] In the *Antidosis*, Isocrates also usefully distinguished deliberation from purely logical reasoning and scientific analysis. And Aristotle equated deliberation with moral reasoning and the creation of practical wisdom (phronesis).[2] This literature shows that people have long understood the distinction between the judgment needed in political decision making and the scientific reasoning needed for questions of fact.

Some of the best examples of what happens in public deliberation have come from the local sponsors of nonpartisan National Issues Forums (NIF).[3] Since the 1980s, thousands of these deliberative forums have been held by schools and colleges, by churches and other religious organizations, by tenant associations, and by humanities councils—even by prisons hoping to return inmates to citizenship. National organizations like the American Bar Association, the Presidential Libraries, and the General Federation of Women's Clubs have also encouraged these deliberations.

These forums deal with disagreements over what is the right thing to do, yet there is seldom, if any, shouting. In a forum using an NIF issue book on AIDS, a participant, convinced that the disease was God's punishment for the wicked, sat in the front row, ready to deliver his message. He had disrupted previous discussions of the issue with his moral pronouncements. In this forum, he was allowed to speak first and he restated his position. But then someone else asked whether there were any others who thought the AIDS issue had a moral dimension. Nearly everyone raised a hand, although few agreed with his position. That drew the first speaker into the group rather than pushing him out. He wasn't the only one who valued moral order. While his point of view didn't change significantly, both the tenor of what he said and the way he participated did. He lowered his voice; he listened more. And after the forum, people commented on how his participation was different from what it had been in less deliberative settings. Conflict remained over which moral imperatives should direct decisions about AIDS policy, yet it was more of a shared conflict, still with a great deal of emotion but less moral posturing.

Have all of the NIF forums been deliberative? No. Sometimes the meetings haven't gone beyond good discussions where everyone is just encouraged to voice their opinions. Yet when participants have dug into making difficult decisions and recognized that painful trade-offs are unavoidable, their collective judgment has become more reflective and shared.[4]

Just for the Well Educated?

Can anyone deliberate or just well-educated people from the middle class? People from all walks of life have been attracted to public deliberations, and there have been no reports of any groups that lacked the capacity for this choice work. For example, Professor Bonnie Braun and a research team at the University of Maryland studied deliberative forums involving women from poor, rural communities. Their research did not show any lack of capacity for deliberating.[5]

It is important to recognize that, while some facilitation can be useful, public deliberation is not one of the many facilitated group processes. It is not a technique to be learned, but rather the exercise of the human faculty for judgment.

Deliberation isn't discussion. "Deliberation" has come to be a word used by many groups for many purposes. The foundation would never claim that it has the only correct definition; Kettering only wants to be clear about what it means by public deliberation.[6]

In recent years, political speech has gotten more attention, partly because it is often bombastic and not civil. Public discussions have been recognized for their ability to connect people with different opinions and promote mutual understanding. Discussions can also bring out information that can lead to a better understanding of complex issues.

Public deliberation has a different purpose, which is to promote shared and sound judgment. That requires dealing with morally grounded disagreements and facing up to difficult trade-offs. The careful weighing that is involved has been described as "choice work" because it is just that, work, and hard work to boot. Even an informed discussion isn't enough to do the job.

EVERYDAY DELIBERATION

Not all deliberation occurs in forums. People make decisions together every day in the political wetlands, and deliberative moments are mixed into ordinary conversations. In fact, public deliberation can only be understood in the larger context of everyday democracy, where citizens act on their problems. Deliberative decision making is necessary in collective action because people have to come to terms with disagreement and conflict. It would be difficult for citizens to act together without deciding together as they act.

In daily life, deliberation is intertwined with acting and isn't a separate process; the experience of acting continually shapes the decision making, just as the decision making shapes the action.[7] For example, as communities try to solve problems, their efforts and the results of those efforts feed into the decision making about how to eliminate the difficulties they face. It makes no sense to think of deliberation as separate from action.

In daily conversations, people talk about the problems that concern them, what action should be taken to respond, and who is needed to act. Yet their conversations may not sound very deliberative. At times people may just be complaining or posturing or looking for someone to blame. Carefully weighing alternatives may be interspersed with comments that don't appear to have anything to do with deliberating. Deliberation isn't a hybrid version of political talk, something apart from ordinary speech. Political speech goes on in multiple layers; people are multitasking. Many of the tasks, however, may be related to deliberation. People may start conversations by telling a story about some troubling experience and then move on to explaining who they are in order to establish their identity. "Don't think I am heartless when I say. . . ."

Even though public, deliberation can't always be heard because the careful weighing of options for action is going on inside people's heads. Deliberation involves listening as much as it does speaking. By listening attentively, we can take in the experiences of others without necessarily agreeing with what they are advocating.

Assuming that people have a capacity for deliberating, the foundation began studying what Jane Mansbridge calls the "deliberative system."[8] This system begins to take shape over backyard fences, during coffee breaks, and at the grocery store. (This is everyday deliberation.) People start by talking to those they live and work with—sometimes including even those who aren't of a like mind. People who look alike don't necessarily think alike. And while some take comfort in opinions they like, they may also be curious about contrary views, provided those views aren't being advanced in an offensive manner. People certainly try to persuade one another as they hold on to cherished beliefs. Yet they may do more; they may begin to weigh the options they like best more carefully.

In deliberation at its best, people recognize the tensions among the things they hold dear and that encourages the careful weighing of various alternatives for action. Without deliberation, discussions easily degenerate into personal pleadings, sound bites, and partisan rancor. Peoples' opinions tend to become store-bought, prepackaged, and unreflective. The public has difficulty teaching itself.

I have already warned against conflating a deliberative forum with deliberation itself because not all forums are deliberative, and deliberation doesn't just happen in forums. That said, deliberative forums can be excellent demonstrations of working through difficult choices. In forums, people can experience what deliberation is like and recognize that it isn't the same as discussion or debate. Often they will say, "we should talk like this more often" or "this is what democracy is like." A forum is a great self-starter for developing a deliberative habit or culture. But it is only a self-starter for deliberative democracy, not the full engine. People have to deliberate more than once to inform their judgment and strengthen their capacity to solve problems.

In this book you will find the terms "deliberation," "public deliberation," "deliberative decision making," and "everyday deliberation." That can be confusing if there is no explanation of why these different terms have been used.

When people use the National Issues Forums guides in their forums, they notice that they don't talk the way they do in most public meetings. Early on, Kettering described this talk as "deliberation." But that raised a problem: juries and legislators deliberate. What was distinctive about what was happening in forums? The forums were citizen-to-citizen or "public deliberation."

The next term, "deliberative decision making," grew out of the need to explain the purpose of public deliberation. Was it just to make people feel better or become more informed? No, the purpose was to make decisions about government policy or civic action. (This decision making is also called "choice work.")

"Everyday deliberation" was introduced to make the point that deliberation isn't confined to small forums. As Amy Gutmann has pointed out, public deliberation belongs everywhere collective decisions are made.[9] Deliberative forums can strengthen what Jane Mansbridge has called the "deliberative system" or what this book calls "everyday deliberation."[10]

CREATING THE KNOWLEDGE WE NEED

A few pages ago, I brought up the subject of how a citizenry informs itself. I want to expand on what I wrote because of the importance conventionally placed on "educating the public." By deliberating, the public creates its own kind of knowledge or practical wisdom (phronesis) about how to act. This is the knowledge that informs public judgment. And it is more than information about local conditions as well as different from the expert knowledge used by professionals.

> The Greeks described the outcome of public deliberations as phronesis. Simply put, it is knowing how to act, knowing what should be done. Phronesis is the sagaciousness or prudence that grows out of purposeful thinking and it ends in resolve to act. In the fourth century, Isocrates provided one of the first accounts of practical wisdom when he distinguished phronesis from scientific knowledge, philosophy, and popular opinion. Isocrates believed that humans had a particular mental faculty that they could use in making political decisions—the ability to distinguish between wise and unwise action, which is captured in the word judgment.[11]

Expert and Public Knowledge

Expert knowledge is technical and scarce; the knowledge people use to decide and act is normative and common: that is, it grows out of everyday experience. Expert knowledge is specific and exclusive; public knowledge is multifaceted and inclusive, as is human experience. Expert knowledge puts a premium on excellence or accuracy; public knowledge puts a premium on applicability or relevance. Both kinds of knowledge are valuable, but they serve different purposes.

Why make so much of these differences? Regrettably, these differences in kinds of knowledge and ways of knowing can be seen as differences between superior and inferior knowledge.[12] Those with expert knowledge are prone to try to "educate" the public with facts alone without regard for what Pericles called the talk that teaches.

Source: CartoonStock.com

I don't want to give the impression that I don't recognize the value of expertise and factual data. I am not a member of the flat earth society. Still, while facts are essential, they can be surrogates for deeply held beliefs. Battles over facts rarely resolve problems because facts aren't the real issue. One of the benefits of deliberation is to surface what is at issue—the tensions among the things we all hold dear, which I've said require the exercise of our best judgment.

Supposedly, expert knowledge is morally neutral or objective, yet experts as professionals have convictions and values—as they should. The difficulty is that values can merge seamlessly into the technical solutions that professionals advocate. Martha Derthick pointed out the differences between professional and lay values in her study of welfare policy.[13] She found that professionals prized uniformity in the application of rules, efficiency in administration, and service without favoritism. Citizens benefit from these values, but people may pay more attention to personal or local circumstances (which vary) and value responsiveness (measured in human terms) more than efficiency. Rules and abstract principles are not as important as common sense, which trumps scientific certainty.

> Public knowledge or practical wisdom is not only different from expert knowledge but also produced in a different way. Knowing how the public should act comes from deliberating, which exercises the human faculty for judgment. In this sense, practical wisdom is socially constructed. Expert or professional knowledge is necessary though not sufficient to produce sound judgments.

DOES PUBLIC DELIBERATION HAVE ANY IMPACT?

The citizens holding NIF forums are often asked whether their deliberations make any difference within the political system. That question implies that the importance of what citizens do is determined by the impact on the state. In other words, what happens in the political wetlands has no value of its own; what happens in institutional policies is all that really matters. The assumption that what happens in government policymaking is the only measure of the worth of public deliberation ignores the importance of the work citizens do with citizens.

In addition, expecting public deliberation to lead to immediate changes in policy ignores the reality of how major policy is informed, which is in a slow, gradual process where numerous forces are at work.[14]

That said, public deliberation's long-term effect on major policy issues has been documented in longitudinal studies such as those cited in *The Rational Public* by Benjamin Page and Robert Shapiro.[15]

Their analysis of responses to a wide variety of policy issues over 50 years showed that the public's attitudes are, on the whole, consistent, rational, and stable.

The public's opinions have proven consistent, this research shows, in that the policies people favor do, over the long term, correspond to what people consider valuable. Page and Shapiro have shown that public attitudes are also rational in that there are clear reasons for them; for example, people favor more spending on employment when unemployment is high. And public preferences are stable in that they change incrementally in understandable responses to changes in circumstances. Why are public policy preferences, over time and on the whole, so consistent, rational, and stable? Page and Shapiro believe that it is because the "cool and deliberate sense of the community" eventually prevails on most issues.

> At the end of the day, the American people are going to have to decide. No president can pursue a policy for very long without the support and the understanding of the Congress and the American people. That's been demonstrated over and over again.
>
> —Dean Rusk[16]

Dan Yankelovich discovered the influence of deliberation in changes in attitudes at the end of certain election campaigns. Widely fluctuating opinions jelled into more stable judgment. That is, attitudes about candidates that initially varied considerably often became more rational, consistent, and stable as the election grew closer. This shift may be the result of everyday deliberation.[17]

Having cited Yankelovich, along with Page and Shapiro, I feel compelled to repeat that I'm not arguing that the public is all-wise. A sound decision is simply one that is consistent with what people consider most valuable. And even a sound decision can, in time, prove to be absolutely wrong headed. The voice of the people isn't the voice of God. Nonetheless, deliberation is beneficial, and the challenge is to reinforce the deliberative sense that exists in the citizenry. That seems a more promising strategy than assuming deliberation is absent, needs to be introduced, and then brought up to scale.

WHEN TO DELIBERATE

Deliberation, for all of its benefits, isn't a cure-all. Deliberative decision making isn't necessary in every situation; there are other valid ways of making choices, such as by negotiating with stakeholders or voting. Deliberative decision making by citizens is only appropriate for certain types of issues.

- Deliberation is useful when citizens are aware of a problem but unsure whether it merits their attention.

- Deliberation helps citizens identify what is deeply valuable that is at stake. Some issues can be decided by accepting or rejecting a technical solution and need not be deliberated by the public. The only caveat is that decisions may be presented in purely technical, professional, or administrative terms, but, in fact, have profound ethical and moral implications.

- Public deliberation is for situations when decisions aren't final. Issues on which a conclusion has already been reached—and the decision makers want public support— are more appropriately presented by advocates arguing the merits of their decision.

- Public deliberation is appropriate for setting policy direction, not for making management decisions. Some issues are in the jurisdiction of a specific agency or institution with a legal obligation to make a decision, an obligation that can't be delegated. Deliberative forums, however, can give officeholders insights into how people go about making up their minds when confronted with painful trade-offs. These insights can be useful when officials are trying to engage the public.

- Public deliberation is most useful to officials at the early stages of setting policy, when the issue has not yet crystallized, or, alternatively, when polarization is threatening to immobilize an agency.

- An issue chosen for deliberative decision making can't be too broad because there are likely to be many issues involved, not just one. Reforming the entire health-care system, for example, is a very broad topic containing many issues, such as constraining costs.

To sum up, public deliberation is most useful on issues that are likely to become divisive unless named and framed in public terms. These issues arise when people are disturbed by what is happening to them yet aren't in agreement about what the problem is or what should be done.

8
FRAMING ISSUES TO
ENCOURAGE DELIBERATION

IF WISE CIVIC ACTION AND GOVERNMENT POLICY DEPEND on sound judgment, and sound judgment requires public deliberation, what could bring public deliberation to bear on urgent issues that burst on the scene? Even if, as Page and Shapiro have found, deliberation slowly changes attitudes over decades, some issues are so urgent that deliberation delayed can be deliberation denied.

Whether or not public deliberation occurs is significantly influenced by how issues are presented or framed. A framework is made up of options for civic action or policy. Options are broad approaches to a problem, not narrow solutions. One option for curbing the high cost of good health care would be to promote more preventive measures. Another option might be to impose price controls.

Framing of some sort goes on all the time. Politicians, professionals in government, special interest groups, and the media frame issues every day. Some frameworks stop deliberation in its tracks: "It's my way or the highway!" "We have a solution that should be adopted immediately, and there aren't any other options worth considering!" "My option is right, and only the morally derelict would oppose it!" Even presenting two options that are polar opposites can trigger adversarial confrontations. (There are seldom only two options for solving a problem.)

Creating a framework to encourage deliberation involves laying out a range of possible actions fairly presented, but this framing in no way restricts people from adding options. In fact, they usually do. Frameworks are just starting points.

To prompt public deliberation, a framework for decision making must accomplish several things: The framework must lay out all the principal options for acting on an issue.[1] These options grow out of the things people value (for example, self-responsibility in the preventive medicine option). Because there are a great many things people care about or that are at stake, there are usually many options to consider. The research done on the National Issues Forums has found that, typically, there are three or four major concerns raised by an issue and so there are usually three or four options that follow.

The options also have to be clear about who would have to act. The government? The schools? The citizenry itself? "We all should" is not realistic; rather, the actors have to be specific people, groups, organizations, or institutions in order for the deliberations to be authentic. Otherwise, the conversations will be about what "they" (some undefined actors) should do.

Each option has to be presented fairly. The way people feel about an option can't be excluded—and shouldn't be. Neuroscientists have found that strong feelings are a necessary complement to rational analysis. Without emotions, reason alone isn't sufficient to guide us.[2] Despite initial concerns that dealing with emotionally charged issues would foster incivility, that hasn't been the case in the NIF deliberations, even on sensitive issues like abortion, AIDS, and race relations. Civility doesn't ensure deliberation, but a deliberative framing seems to encourage it.

If the issue isn't presented fairly, many people will resist what they see as an attempt to manipulate them. And in order to be fair, the framing has to include the advantages as well as the disadvantages of each option. The advantages and disadvantages can't be purely practical considerations like costs and efficiency; they have to reflect what people consider valuable.

Because deliberation takes into account the things people hold dear, the descriptions of the advantages and disadvantages have to be clear about which concerns would be eased by an option and which would be exacerbated. "Would this option make us more or less secure?" "Would we be freer or more restricted?" "Would this option be fair?" In other words, the framework for decision making has to identify the tensions among the many things we hold dear.

Unless people are aware of the tensions, they tend to ignore them. Why risk more conflict in an already contentious society? Yet if tensions are repressed, they may well reemerge to block civic work. As I said, communities can bog down in solution wars as advocates bombard one another with facts that serve as surrogates for values. It is better to confront and work through the tensions rather than expect they will disappear and everyone will agree (which rarely occurs). Presenting the tensions up front makes clear what is really at issue and requires deliberating.

The purpose of a deliberative framing is to help people get to the point where they are able to move ahead in solving a problem, even though not in full agreement. That is, deliberation helps create a common ground for action. Common ground for action is not the same as full accord; it's just the pragmatic basis for combating a contentious issue. This "ground" is the arena of the politically permissible, the area bounded by what the public will not support. For example, in NIF deliberations on offensive material on the Internet, participants favored some constraints but not government censorship.[3]

A deliberative framing should also make us more aware that we not only differ with one another, but also within ourselves. We are conflicted individually as well as collectively because each of us holds a great many things dear and they, too, clash.

When we recognize our internal conflicts, we become more open to the views of others. As long as we are convinced we are absolutely right, we have little incentive to listen seriously to what others say. (I'll have more about how this recognition helps in problem solving in the next chapter.)

While people in positions of authority may frame issues in partisan or expert terms, there isn't any reason citizens can't frame issues in their own terms to promote deliberation. In fact, citizens can and have framed many issues for deliberation, particularly on local issues.[4] Ruth's Indigenous Issues Forums that were cited early on are a good example.

As people deliberate, they often revise what they discover were faulty framings. Framing issues, like naming problems, goes on as people deliberate to reach some common ground for action. In fact, renaming and reframing are integral to deliberating.

WHAT FRAMING SHOULD DO

In order to promote deliberation, framing an issue should have these characteristics:

- The things that concern people—that they consider valuable—should be reflected in the options for action, and the actions should follow logically from people's concerns.

- The advantages and disadvantages of each option, which require making trade-offs, should be clear. And the framework should not lend itself to selecting "all of the above" because that avoids confronting and working through the tensions that arise from having to make trade-offs.

- The consequences that might follow from actions to solve a problem should also be described in terms of their effects on the things people hold dear, not just in practical terms of costs and feasibility.

- The actors who need to act should include citizens working together (not just as individuals). The framework should also recognize governmental, nongovernmental, and for-profit actors.

- Each option must be presented "best foot forward"; that is, in the most positive light. Negative consequences should be described with equal fairness. This ensures the "fair trial" that people look for.

- An effective framework should recognize unpopular points of view.

- The pros of one option are not the cons of another. Each option needs to be considered in light of its own advantages and disadvantages. Otherwise, the framing truncates the process of decision making.

- An effective framework should not prompt the usual conversations; it should disrupt old patterns and open new conversations. So a framework for public deliberation should not replicate the prevailing academic, professional, or partisan framework. It must reflect where citizens are in thinking about an issue, wherever that may be; it should start where people start.

- An effective framework often leaves people stewing because they become more aware of the undesirable effects of the options they like most. The tensions or trade-offs must be clear, authentic, and unavoidable because they are needed to produce the learning that choice work is intended to prompt.

I can't overemphasize the importance of frameworks that will create an environment for shared learning. Deliberative frameworks or issue books that serve as guides to deliberation aren't created to simplify complex issues but rather to underscore the perplexity that is generated by tensions among and within options, and by the need to make difficult trade-offs. This perplexity is the agitation that prompts learning that informs actions.

IMPLICATIONS FOR CIVIC ENGAGEMENT

Creating a framework for decision making, which begins with naming issues to reflect people's primary concerns, has particular implications for institutions and civic organizations that want to engage other citizens. They may need public support or legitimacy; or they have to meet legislated engagement mandates; or they just want to raise the level of public participation in their community.

Kettering's view of civic engagement has been influenced by watching citizens name and frame issues in preparation for or during deliberative forums. The foundation's first insight has been that, rather than assuming people are indifferent and uninvolved, engagement efforts could start with what already engages people, which is with what they consider most valuable. Connecting with citizens in this way doesn't involve drawing them out of their personal lives into politics. Consistent with that insight, institutional leaders may be better served by going to where people already congregate rather than depending on citizens to show up for called meetings. This kind of engagement connects personal concerns with public issues.

Unfortunately, many engagement efforts start where the organizers start—with *their* names for issues, with *their* framework for decision making, and with *their* answers to the problems at hand. I'll say again, these efforts may result in a persuaded populace but not in a truly engaged and responsible citizenry.

The foundation also has come to see that the public isn't just a static body like an audience or the names in the telephone directory. When people are engaged as citizens, they move around. They're busy relating to one another. They work together. The public can be thought of as a dynamic force, not just a static body. Thinking of the public as more like electricity than a light bulb focuses attention on the sources of political energy. Not being static, this in-motion public can't be represented by any one person or a select group.

The implication of this insight is that civic engagement should connect to the dynamics of civic work and not just engage individuals.

What institutions and civic organizations do could be more aligned with what citizens do, which would give them the benefits of civic work and also make that work more effective. I'll say more about what this work is in the next chapter.

For now, I want to recall an earlier reference to what philosophers call "the political." The dynamic public isn't out there and apart from us. It's interactive—both within each of us and among us. We are not, by our nature, politicians; but we are, by nature, political beings. There is a political dimension to our everyday lives; it is in what we do with others. And everyday life is filled with opportunities for citizens to make a difference.

9
OPPORTUNITIES IN COMMUNITIES

IF THE PUBLIC TO BE ENGAGED is a citizenry-in-motion, a citizenry working together to solve common problems and create a better life, where can it be found? Xavier de Souza Briggs thinks it is in communities.[1] I believe he is right, even though we all recognize that communities also have conditions in them that can keep people from joining with one another. Citizens disagree on what their problems are and what is the right thing to do about them. They worry that they don't have the resources needed to act effectively. They organize a multitude of projects that move in different directions and fail to reinforce one another. They learn little from their efforts; civic momentum fails before much has been accomplished. These are all symptoms of problems of democracy.

When I say "communities," I mean placed-based, geographic communities—neighborhoods, towns, cities, counties—the places where people live, work, and raise families. These communities are constellations of small groups with quite different interests and outlooks. They aren't homogeneous.

To be sure, there are many other kinds of communities, and most of us belong to several. Some communities aren't place-based, such as those on the Internet. But I am talking about geographic communities, because what happens in them affects the long-term vitality of the

Illustration by Jennifer Berman

*Democracy must begin at home, and its home
is the neighborly community.*

—John Dewey[2]

economy, the health of residents, the education of children, the degree
of resilience in the face of natural disasters, and more.

These communities need not be parochial enclaves; changes made
in them may start locally but not be confined to the neighborhoods
where they began. Change can and does radiate out.[3] It begins in a
shared sense that people joined together can get things done, which is
called "collective efficacy."

Robert Sampson found that

> in neighborhoods that are otherwise similar, those with higher
> levels of collective efficacy exhibit lower rates of crime, not just
> in the present, but in the following years. . . . collective efficacy

is relatively stable over time and . . . predicts future variations in crime, adjusting for the aggregated characteristics of individuals and more traditional forms of neighbor networks (e.g., friend/kinship ties). More important, highly efficacious communities seem to do better on a lot of other things, including birth weight, rates of teen pregnancy, and infant mortality, suggesting a link to overall health and wellbeing independent of social composition. In most cases, then, whether rich or poor, white or black . . . collective efficacy signals a community on a trajectory of wellbeing.[4]

DOING THE WORK OF DEMOCRACY

If community well-being is related to a habit of working together, people's inability to join together is a serious problem, not only for a community, but also for democracy. This chapter describes ways that citizens go about the work that put more control in their hands, and it identifies opportunities to do the work.

I think of ways of working that empower citizens as "democratic practices." I chose the word "practices" to make a distinction. Practices are more than techniques in that they have a value in themselves. There are techniques for hammering nails efficiently, but hammering has little value beyond the activity itself. Playing the piano, on the other hand, has a worth beyond striking a string; the playing has a value in itself. It is a practice.

Sadly, opportunities to employ democratic practices often go unrecognized. This reinforces the fear that people can't make a difference in solving problems, a fear sometimes called by a fancy name—a loss of agency—which is the opposite of collective efficacy.

In saying that people have more opportunities to shape the future than they may recognize, I am not implying that anything is possible if people would just cooperate a little more and pull themselves up by their bootstraps. While much of what people need to make a difference is in their communities, not everything is. And citizens aren't all powerful when put up against the power of wealth or impersonal forces like globalization. Still, citizens could benefit from an array of empowering resources if they recognize their potential and the opportunities to use it.

SUGGSVILLE: PRACTICING THE PRACTICES

An earlier chapter discusses several of the opportunities I am talking about, and one is in something quite ordinary—selecting a name for a problem. What name is given to a problem, and who does the naming, aren't insignificant; naming and framing are opportunities.

The foundation found these opportunities by observing scores of communities. But individual cases, taken by themselves, didn't convey the significance of what we were seeing. So I have made a trade-off in presenting what Kettering learned. While sacrificing some of the authenticity of individual stories, I have created a composite town—an avatar—called Suggsville.[5] Not wanting to claim that the foundation had found perfect communities to use as models, I based the Suggsville composite on places we had seen where conditions were less than ideal in order to emphasize the difficulties citizens encounter in doing their work.

Naming Problems to Capture What Is Most Valuable to Citizens

Suggsville was and still is rural and poor. Once a prosperous farming community, the town began to decline during the 1970s as the agricultural economy floundered. By the 1990s, the unemployment rate soared above 40 percent. Property values plummeted. With little else to replace the income from idle farms, a drug trade flourished. A majority of Suggsville's children were born to single teenagers. The schools were plagued with low test scores and troubling dropout rates. Disease rates were higher than in most communities; obesity was becoming epidemic, and alcoholism was pervasive. Nearly everyone who could leave the town had, especially college-educated young adults. Making matters worse, the community was sharply divided: rich and poor, black and white.

After church services and in the one grocery store that survived, Suggsvillians discussed what was happening with friends and neighbors. Different groups made small talk and mulled over the town's difficulties, but no decisions were made or actions taken. Then consultants from the state land-grant university who had been asked to advise made a modest suggestion—begin a town meeting where citizens could assess their situation and decide what they might do. Initially, the consultants' proposed meeting drew the predictable handful. People sat in racially homogeneous clusters—until someone rearranged the chairs into a circle and citizens began to mingle. After participants got off their favorite soapboxes, told their own stories, and stopped looking for others to blame, they eventually settled down to identifying the problems that concerned everyone. Economic security was at the top of the list, but it wasn't the only concern. Crime was another.

As the town meetings continued—slowly, sometimes haltingly— Suggsvillians laid out a number of concerns reflecting the things they valued. People didn't choose one issue and discard all the others. The need to restore economic well-being was just the first name for the town's problem, and it resonated with other concerns like family instability. The social structure and moral order seemed to be crumbling and people felt insecure.

As people added names for problems, they implicated themselves in solving them. They could do something about the alcoholism that was threatening both families and the social order. And they could do something about the children who suffered when adults took little responsibility for their well-being. Naming was an opportunity to regain a sense of agency.

If the Suggsville story were on video, I would pause here and explain that the town meeting and the other casual conversations were an opportunity for citizens to have a stronger hand in shaping their future. Their problems could be named in terms that resonated with the things they valued.[6]

It isn't difficult to find out what people consider valuable. Just ask them how a problem affects them and their family or what is at stake. Naming a problem in terms of what people hold dear (in public terms) isn't, however, simply describing it in everyday language. When people talk about what's at stake, they bring up concerns that are deeply important to most everyone. I cited some of these—being secure from danger, being free to pursue one's own interests, being treated fairly by others.

Problems aren't always named, however, in terms of what is valuable to citizens; they are more likely to be given expert names by professionals, or institutional leaders and the media. There isn't anything wrong with that as such; expert names are usually technically accurate. The unfortunate result is that these names seldom reflect the more intangible things that people care deeply about. For example, people are more likely to relate to poverty when it is named in the way they see it, which is as hunger. The result of these differences is that people don't necessarily feel any connection to issues that those in positions of authority consider important. These leaders then interpret this lack of connection as public indifference.

Expert names, particularly when used by schools and government agencies, can also suggest that there is little citizens can do about a problem. Consequently, people are disinclined to get involved because they don't see how they can make a difference. For instance, invitations from an economic development organization encouraging citizens to participate in solving a problem may sound hollow if the problem has been named in a way that doesn't relate to what people value.

Institutions eager to engage citizens might take note: naming problems in terms the public uses can facilitate the deepest kind of civic engagement because the names that reflect people's deepest concerns encourage them to own their problems. Owning problems is a potent source of energy for civic work.

Framing Issues to Identify All the Options— and the Tensions in Them

Given concerns about the economy, one of the first proposals in what had become a series of Suggsville town meetings was to recruit a manufacturing company. The suggestion stayed on the table, although some participants had a practical objection—every other town in the state was competing for new industries. Some development authorities had recommended a grow-your-own business strategy, but not convinced that this was a good recommendation, a few who felt strongly about recruiting new industry left the group and went to the state office of economic development for assistance. Nonetheless, the majority of the participants continued to discuss the recommendation to encourage local businesses. Several mentioned a restaurant that had opened recently; it promised to stimulate a modest revival downtown. Unfortunately, that promise wasn't being realized because unemployed men (and youngsters who liked to hang out with them) were congregating on the street in front of the restaurant—and drinking. Customers shied away.

At this point in the Suggsville meetings, having heard everyone's concerns, their visions for the town's future, and the actions they might take, there was an opportunity to create an inclusive framework for the decisions needed to make visions into realities. As said earlier, public decision making is best served by a framework that includes all the major options (which are based on what people consider valuable) and also identifies tensions among the things people hold dear. Recognizing these tensions is critical in dealing with disagreements.

If framing is key to dealing with disagreements, how does it occur in real time? The everyday question, "If you are that concerned, what do you think should be done?" can start the process. As happened in Suggsville, people typically respond by talking about both their concerns and the actions they favor. The concerns are implicit in the suggestions for action.

People's concerns, and there are usually many, will generate a variety of specific proposals for action. That certainly happened in Suggsville when the issue was what to do about the faltering economy. The people in the town meetings suggested numerous courses of action to revive the economy. Most everyone had first assumed that the problem was a lack of jobs, but that diagnosis changed as other concerns pointed to other problems.

Even though each course of action is different, they often center around one basic concern. In this case, it was the economy, so the various actions to stimulate growth were actually all part of one option. An option is made up of actions that have the same purpose or move in the same direction.

Actions like attracting industry, encouraging startup companies, and supporting local businesses are all about creating new jobs. Other options that emerged from the meetings included creating a better place to live with actions like improving the schools, providing more programs for young people, and reducing crime. Economic development was defined as greater prosperity, not just jobs.

A framework that recognizes the major concerns and lays out the options that follow from them (along with the various actions and actors that have to be involved) sets the stage for a fair trial. For a trial to be truly fair, each option has to be presented with its best foot forward, as well as with its drawbacks.

A fair trial in public decision making engages tensions rather than avoiding them. As people wrestle with options for acting on a problem, they often find themselves pulled and tugged in different directions. These tensions invariably arouse strong feelings, and nothing will make these emotions disappear. On the other hand, if the framing begins by recognizing what citizens value, people may realize that their differences are over the means to the same ends. (The example I've used before is that we all value security and freedom, although we differ on how to balance the two.) This recognition has the potential to change the tone of the disagreements. The conversation opens up and becomes less dogmatic.

> Disagreement per se isn't a problem of democracy; it's ingrained in human nature and can't be solved or eliminated. In fact, a certain level of disagreement is essential in a democracy because a diversity of opinion protects against "group think" and the errors that it leads to. The problem is how disagreement is dealt with. Inevitable tensions over what is the right thing to do aren't always recognized and worked through. That's the problem that undermines democracy.

When we realize that we are pulled in different directions personally, we may become less absolute in our opinions and more attentive to the views of others, even those with whom we disagree. This openness allows us to see problems from different perspectives, which gives us a more complete view of them. This expanded understanding is crucial to effective problem solving. Redefining problems allows us to think anew about how to combat them.

Deliberating Publicly to Make Sound Decisions

At the next Suggsville town meeting, attendance was higher. Some members of the town council and a few other officials began to participate. Participants knew what was at stake: nothing less than the life of the community. They began talking about what could be done to save the restaurant. Initially, the conversation was about who to blame for the restaurant's difficulties. The police chief argued that the problem was loitering and recommended stricter enforcement of ordinances. Others weren't so sure. Strict enforcement, even if it worked to clear the streets, could give the community the appearance of a police state. Could people live with these consequences?

Still others worried about problems they thought contributed to the loitering. One woman suggested that loitering was symptomatic of widespread alcoholism. As citizens put their concerns on the table, they struggled with what was most important to the welfare of the community. People valued a great many things. The Suggsville that they hoped to create would be family friendly and safe for kids. It would have good schools as well as a strong economy.

Yet everything that would have to be done to reach those objectives had potential downsides, as was the case with stricter law enforcement. Tensions were unavoidable. People had to decide what was really most valuable to the community. They seemed ready to weigh the potential consequences of different options against the things they held dear.

Step outside Suggsville again and look at the opportunity to turn a discussion into public deliberations that would weigh various options against all the things people held dear. The door was open to raise questions in the meeting like, "if we did what you suggest, and it worked—yet also had negative consequences—would you still stand by your proposal?"

The work of deliberative decision making—choice work—occurs in stages, never all at once.[7] One town meeting or forum isn't enough. Stages aren't steps in a sequence but points along the way in an evolving process. Initially, in some communities, citizens may not be sure whether there is an issue they should be concerned about. In the first stage, people have to decide if anything dear to them is at stake. A bit later, they may become aware of a problem that touches on something they value, yet simply gripe about it. The "issue" is who to blame. At this stage, people may not see the tensions or the necessity for citizens to act. When the tensions do become apparent, people usually struggle as they weigh the advantages and disadvantages of various options. Eventually, citizens may work through an issue and settle on a range of actions that move in a common direction.

Seeing the public move through these stages caused Dan Yankelovich to realize that a democratic citizenry has a learning curve. That is, people don't simply gather information and come to a new understanding of a problem. Their understanding evolves, often moving in spurts rather than along a smooth trajectory. The point is that the public can learn—perhaps not quickly and certainly not perfectly—but more often than not.[8]

These stages have important implications for institutional leaders and officeholders. Knowing where citizens are (and aren't) in their thinking is crucial for engaging them. When citizens aren't sure there is a problem, leaders may be well advised to start where people start, even though experts may have moved on in their thinking. Citizens may not be ready to consider solutions at this point. The issue that has to be addressed is the *nature* of the issue; what exactly is at issue?

When people do, indeed, recognize there is a serious issue, yet still look for a scapegoat, revisiting the nature of the problem seems likely to be more helpful than officials pounding away at the solution they favor. Even when citizens move past blaming, they may be unsure of what their options are and what trade-offs they will have to make. At that stage, they are susceptible to being polarized, particularly if politicians engage in a hard-sell strategy. However, once people reach the point of struggling with trade-offs, they are more likely to be open to information that is relevant to their concerns.

When a citizenry does finally settle on a general direction to move, they don't produce a set of instructions for officials to carry out, but officials should have a clearer sense of what the citizenry will or won't support. In some cases, officials will think that the best course of action is outside the boundaries of what is politically permissible. In these situations, public deliberations can tell officeholders how the citizenry went about making up its mind so officials can engage this thinking when they believe it errs.

Identifying and Committing Resources

As people in Suggsville were working through tensions, some civic groups were already taking action or planning to. Deciding and acting were intertwined. Worried that there were too many youngsters with too little adult supervision, several community organizations responded with offers of things they were willing to do if others would join them: organize baseball and softball leagues, provide after-school classes, expand youth services in the churches, form a band. The observation that alcoholism was contributing to the town's difficulties prompted other participants in the meetings to propose that a chapter of Alcoholics Anonymous be established. Where would it meet? Someone offered a vacant building free of charge. As more projects developed and citizens called on others to join them, new recruits began coming to the meetings. Rather than deciding on a single solution, people mounted an array of initiatives that were loosely coordinated because the initiatives were reasonably consistent with the sense of direction that was emerging from the deliberations.

Because decisions aren't self-implementing, Suggsvillians were busy identifying and committing resources. As people came to see their economic problems more clearly, resources that had been unrecognized or seemed irrelevant took on new significance. The same was true of the people and organizations that control those resources. Suggsvillians who knew how to coach youngsters to play baseball weren't an asset until community revitalization was seen as more than a strictly economic problem.

The resources needed to implement a decision are sometimes hidden in unlikely places. In one of the poorest sections of Suggsville, some people were concerned about what their youngsters were (and weren't) learning. The congregation of a nearby church responded. Members found resources for improving education among the very people typically thought to have little to offer—even those with little education. They discovered these resources by asking a series of questions: What do you know how to do well? Where did you learn it? What helped you learn it? Have you ever taught anyone anything? What do you think made your teaching effective?[9] People's first reaction was, "I never taught anybody anything," perhaps because they associated teaching with classrooms. Later, however, they described numerous ways in which they had, in fact, educated others. They had taught basic skills like cooking, sewing, and taking care of equipment. Their "lessons" included the virtues of patience, persistence, and sacrifice. Such resources are genuine assets; they help solve problems. And when people recognize they have these resources, it gives them a sense of agency, of being able to make a difference.

In order for citizens to see themselves as actors, recognizing their resources can be prompted early on in framings to promote deliberation by identifying all potential actors. Institutions—governments, schools, hospitals, and major NGOs—are obvious actors; yet while necessary, they are seldom enough to deal with a community's most persistent problems, which come from many sources and require some response from every sector of a community.

Unfortunately, in many communities these local resources are never identified; institutional politics has taken over. Citizens may have named and framed an issue, but professionals can step in, unintentionally pushing citizens out. Institutions tend to rely on familiar routines like strategic planning, which doesn't normally have provisions for civic work. Professionals often assume that once people have spoken, it's time for citizens to step back and for professionals to follow up with their resources.

Another reason the work citizens can do with citizens is overlooked is that institutional and political leaders have been frustrated in trying to engage people, as reported before. Furthermore, institutions have money and legal authority; they can rely on enforceable contracts. The democratic public can't command people or deploy equipment, and it seldom has any legal authority.

Illustration by Jennifer Berman

I believe in democracy because it releases the energies of every human being.

—Woodrow Wilson[10]

Then why do people do things like organizing rescue parties after natural disasters when there is no financial inducement or legal obligation? After all, entering a devastated neighborhood isn't just time consuming; it can be dangerous. Often people will commit to such an effort and carry out what they've promised to do if their commitments are made public. Their fellow citizens will expect it of them. (Recall the power of covenants.) These commitments are reinforced when others promise to use their resources. Norms of reciprocity come into play. As happened in Suggsville, it isn't uncommon for deliberative decision making to be followed by mutual promises to commit resources, either at public forums or subsequent meetings.

Organizing Complementary Acting

As civic work in Suggsville progressed, several people returned to the argument that, while encouraging local businesses was fine, it would never provide enough jobs to revive the economy. The town still had to attract outside investment, they insisted. Someone quickly pointed out that the center of town, especially the park, was so unsightly that no one of sound mind would consider Suggsville an attractive location for a new business. Even though some saw little connection between the condition of the park and recruiting industry, no one denied that the town needed a facelift. Suggsville's three-member sanitation crew, however, had all it could do to keep up with garbage collection. Did people feel strongly enough about the cleanup to accept the consequences? Would they show up to clean the park themselves? In the past, responses to similar calls had been minimal. This time, after one of the community forums, a group of people committed to gathering at the park the following Saturday with rakes, mowers, and trash bags.

During most of these community meetings, the recently elected mayor sat quietly, keeping an eye on what was happening. The forums had begun during his predecessor's administration, and the town's new leader felt no obligation to them. In fact, he was a bit suspicious of what the participants were doing. Members of the town council feared the public meetings would result in just another pressure group. But no one made any demands on the town government, although some citizens thought it strange that the mayor hadn't offered to help with the cleanup. Then, before Saturday arrived, people were surprised to find that the mayor had sent workers to the park with trucks and other heavy equipment to do what the tools brought from home couldn't.

Opportunities for the citizenry to act emerge as people decide on common directions and shared purposes. This is what happened in Suggsville. Just as the public has its own distinctive resources, it also has its own distinctive way of organizing action and acting. Government agencies act on behalf of the public, and people act individually by volunteering for all sorts of civic projects. Both are beneficial; neither is the public acting. When a citizenry acts, different groups launch an armada of small initiatives.

Although the citizenry acts in a variety of ways, these initiatives reinforce one another when they have a shared sense of direction or purpose, which can emerge from public deliberations. The result—

complementary acting by citizens—is not only multifaceted but also mutually reinforcing; various civic efforts "complete" one another. This is different from cooperation coordinated by civic organizations. Complementary civic action employs people's capacity for self-organizing.

Human beings seem to have a capacity for organizing themselves, a capacity most evident when natural disasters sweep away all avenues for outside assistance.[11] Self-organizing among people not kin to or alike one another probably dates back to the time before there were chiefdoms; a time when there was little hierarchy but a need for self-organizing in order to survive. That was long before the Greeks coined the term "democracy."[12]

While complementary acting requires a degree of coordination (everyone should show up to clean up the park on the same day), it isn't administratively regulated and doesn't have administrative expenses. This means that the cost of getting things done is usually lower than institutional costs.

The payoff from complementary public acting goes beyond the tangible products of civic work. As research showed, the work people do together like cleaning up a park is valued, not just because the park is nicer, but because it demonstrates that people joining forces can make a difference.[13] And when people work together, they get a more realistic sense of what they can expect from one another. This is political trust, which isn't quite the same as personal trust and shouldn't be confused with it. Political trust can develop among people who aren't family or friends. All that is necessary is for citizens to recognize they need one another to solve their community's problems. That recognition builds pragmatic relationships.[14]

The ability of complementary acting to supplement rather than substitute for institutional action has long been recognized in research on urban reform. For instance, Clarence Stone has reported that people and institutions that form alliances in city neighborhoods accomplish far more than any institution alone could.[15] Institutions should have little difficulty in encouraging complementary acting when they value and make a place for it. The Squares and the Blobs need each other!

Learning as a Community

Although the restaurant held its own, new industry didn't come to Suggsville. Drug traffic continued to be a problem, yet people's vigilance, together with more surveillance by the police department, reduced the trade. The crowd loitering on the streets dwindled away. More people attended the A.A. meetings even though alcoholism remained an issue. A new summer recreation program became popular with young people, and teenage pregnancies decreased a bit, as did high school dropout rates.

In time, the ad hoc Suggsville improvement group became an official civic association. As might be expected, the organization had the usual internal disputes that detracted from community problem solving. Still, when a controversy was brewing in the community or an emerging issue needed to be addressed, citizens used the association to bring people together.

Some projects didn't work. In most instances, when that happened, association members adjusted their sights and launched more initiatives. Perhaps this momentum had something to do with the way the association involved the community in evaluating projects. The association regularly convened meetings where citizens could reflect on what the community had learned, regardless of whether the projects succeeded. Success wasn't as important as the lessons that could be used in future efforts.

Suggsville had become a learning community.[16] In this collective or public learning, the citizenry or community itself learns, and the learning is reflected in changed behavior. Suggsville, for example, changed the way it did business when the town meetings took hold. The founders moved on and the membership fluctuated, but the improvement association that sponsored the forums was still operating years after it was formed.

There are obviously a great many opportunities for a citizenry to learn after a community has acted on a problem. Everyone wants to know whether the effort has succeeded. The press declares the results to be beneficial, harmful, or inconsequential. One-on-one conversations bubble up in the grocery store. Outside evaluators make "objective" assessments. The citizenry, however, may not learn a great deal from the media's conclusions, chance conversations, or professional evaluations.

One reason the citizenry doesn't learn can be the unintentional interference from certain types of conventional, outcome-based evaluations using neutral evaluators. In order for a community to learn, people have to focus on themselves as a community. The evidence to be evaluated can't just be what projects have achieved; it has to include how well citizens have worked together. That said, public learning could supplement the outcome-based assessments that are often required by funders.

Public learning is distinctive in that the results aren't just measured against fixed, predetermined goals. When a democratic citizenry learns, both the objectives of civic efforts and their results have to be on the table for inspection, not just the results alone. As people learn, they may realize that what they first thought was most valuable turned out not to be as important as it seemed initially.

Opportunities for public learning aren't confined to final evaluations; they can occur all along as citizens do their work. To name an issue in public terms is to learn what others value. To frame an issue is to learn about all of the options for action—as well as the tensions that need to be worked through. To decide deliberatively is to learn which actions are consistent or inconsistent with what is held most valuable. To identify resources is to learn what resources are relevant, and where potential allies might be found. To organize complementary action is to learn which initiatives can reinforce one another.

In many ways, public learning is renaming, reframing, and deciding again—after the fact. It is deliberation in reverse. The questions are much the same: Should we have done what we did? Was it really consistent with what we now think is most important?

The greatest benefit of public learning is an increase in civic capacity as a result of what Hannah Arendt, drawing upon the German philosopher Immanuel Kant, called an "enlarged mentality," the ability to see things from others' points of view.[17] Public learning develops a citizenry's capacity for seeing new possibilities in life. You might say it improves civic eyesight.

Learning communities are like the ideal student who reads everything assigned and then goes to the library or searches the Internet to find out more. These communities don't copy a model or use a formula. Rather than trying to follow best practices, learning communities study what others have done but adapt what they see to their own circumstances. They create better practices.

Community projects that aim primarily for immediate success tend to end when their goals have been met. This can occur even if problems remain. On the other hand, projects that don't succeed disappoint citizens, and they, too, stop. So success and failure can have the same result: people may quit in either case. When communities are learning, they tend to push ahead because they look beyond success and failure. As Rudyard Kipling wrote, they "treat those two imposters just the same."[18] If the work in learning communities goes well, people try to improve on it. If the work fails, they learn from their mistakes.

Learning by and in a community is more than acquiring and disseminating information. It is more than evaluating civic efforts. It is a mindset about change and progress, an attitude that is open to experimentation and reflective in the face of failure. "If at first you don't succeed, try, try again." And if you do succeed, raise the bar and aim higher. Public learning is a political mindset that makes for a democratic culture.

WHAT HAPPENED?

Attendance at the Suggsville association meetings continued to rise and fall depending on which problems were being addressed. Some association members worried about these fluctuations; others thought getting people to come to meetings was less important than building ties with other civic groups and rural neighborhood coalitions, as well as with

*institutions like the county law enforcement agencies, the economic
development office, and the health department. Creating networks was
a priority. Several people dropped out because they wanted the association to play a more partisan role. But the association refused to get
drawn into local election campaigns or to endorse special causes.*

*Suggsville wouldn't make anyone's list of model communities today;
still, the town has changed: citizens have a greater ability to influence
their future. Asked what the years of civic work produced, one Suggsvil-
lian said it was learning how to work together.*

BUILDING ON WHAT GROWS

Much of the progress in Suggsville was based on making use of what
was already happening or capitalizing on potentials waiting to be realized. All of the practices used to do the work of citizens were adapted
from familiar routines. People were already talking about how the
town's problems were affecting them. They were already thinking
about what should be done and about their options. The town meetings just put these efforts to use in renaming and reframing issues so
that citizens could be involved on their own terms.

Many of the resources needed to combat some of the town's problems were available in unlikely places, even in the educating that
people with little formal schooling could provide. As John McKnight
and John Kretzmann have shown, identifying untapped assets can be
more powerful than focusing on needs.[19] Suggsville's greatest accomplishment was in seeing the potential in what already existed. In a
town that could have been defined by what it couldn't do, people were
able to show that there were some things they could do. Certainly not
entirely alone, certainly not without some outside help, the towns-
people started essentially within. They may not have used the phrase
"collective efficacy," but they had it. Eventually, Suggsville changed
its political culture—changed the way it went about its business. You

might say that it developed an asset-based democracy with a strategy of starting with what was already happening or available nearby.

It is also significant that the practices used in the town weren't separate, stand-alone efforts. Rather, they fit together much like the *matrëška* nesting dolls from Russia. This coherence made it possible to bring about a new way of doing business. When people laid out their options for acting on a problem, they continued to mull over the name that best captured what was really at issue. Even as they moved toward making a decision, they kept revising both the framework and the name of the problem. As they deliberated, people anticipated the actions that would need to be taken and the commitments they might have to make. They recalled lessons learned from past efforts. Citizens made commitments to act while they were still deliberating, and they deliberated while they were still acting. They were also learning all along the way.

Illustration by Jennifer Berman

Build on what grows.

—J. Herman Blake[20]

10
DEMOCRATIC PRACTICES

THE SUGGSVILLE STORY illustrates six democratic practices that give citizens a stronger hand in shaping their future. They are ways of doing the work people must do if they are to rule themselves. I would say again that the practices aren't separate activities but rather interrelated efforts in a different way of doing politics.

I hesitated to make the practices into a chart because I was afraid it would give the impression that the practices were another of the numerous techniques or skill sets used to facilitate group processes or engage people in planning exercises. Practices aren't tools; they promote democratic values and stimulate the learning that allows citizens to combat many of their own problems. They are ways of both learning and doing simultaneously. Here are six that seem essential:

1. Naming problems to reflect the things people consider valuable and hold dear, not expert information alone.

2. Framing issues for decision making that not only takes into account what people value but also lays out all the major options for acting fairly and with full recognition of the tension growing out of advantages and disadvantages of each option.

3. Making decisions deliberatively to move opinions from first impressions to more shared and reflective judgment.

4. Identifying and committing civic resources, assets that often go unrecognized and unused.

5. Organizing civic actions so they complement one another, which makes the whole of people's efforts more than the sum of the parts.

6. Learning as a community all along the way to keep up civic momentum.

The practices, taken together, are a response to the questions raised in every community facing troubling circumstances. People want to know how *they* can come together as a community—despite their differences—to sustain their community. They aren't asking for the name of a person or organization that will give them answers. They are asking how *they* can find their own answers. One place to look is at the opportunities to do business-as-usual politics differently.

POLITICAL SPACE WITHOUT A STREET ADDRESS

The politics that emerges from the six democratic practices doesn't have a distinctive location. Usually people have to go to specially designated places to practice "politics": the voting booth or the jury box. Democratic practices, on the other hand, can begin almost anywhere. I've used coffee shops, grocery stores, and even kitchen tables as examples. Nearly all of the places where people regularly gather can provide public space, although the places with the most opportunities are those that are open to more than one congregation, class, constituency, or membership.

I would also suggest that practicing democratic practices creates its own space. There is no street address; the space appears whenever people take advantage of opportunities to go about familiar routines in a more democratic way. Notice how much space opened up whenever and wherever choices were being made in Suggsville. The act of choosing transforms ordinary space into public space.

I would add that choosing embodies a powerful democratic idea. To recognize that we can choose even the smallest things empowers us, makes us responsible, and liberates us from the oppressive thought that we are helpless in the face of forces beyond our control. A community is the product of choices made over time, even the choices made by not choosing.

I can't write about opportunities for democratic practices, however, without acknowledging the obstacles to changing existing routines into practices. Practicing the practices can also be challenging.

BUT CITIZENS CAN'T

The claim that the work done by citizens can make a difference not only runs up against arguments that most people have neither the ability nor the will to be democratic citizens, but also runs up against deeply entrenched notions of what is required to make significant change in a society. And the citizens I introduced in the beginning of the book, the Ruths and Genes, encounter two other barriers. One is the argument that their work seldom gets up to enough size or scope to produce meaningful change. The other barrier is a mindset that only leaders, not citizens, are the ones who make real change.

I would not reject these criticisms out of hand. Yet democratic practices, like deliberative decision making, extend their reach by creating networks and by influencing existing, large-scale systems of communication. And while leaders with initiative are essential, democratic practices foster a civic style of leadership that can make communities *leaderful*.

It has also been argued that certain conditions have to be present in order for democracy and its practices to exist. For instance, it has been said that there has to be a civil atmosphere, mutual understanding, and trust. Certainly the absence of any of these is a barrier to democratic practices. But civility, mutual understanding, and trust aren't preconditions; they are byproducts of democratic practices.

The product itself is a democratic public. In other words, the practices create a democratic public. The practices are a democratic public in motion.

Up to Scale?

If democratic practices are confined to a few meetings and aren't tied together, they would be of such a limited scale that they couldn't have a significant impact.[1] That said, I think the not-up-to-scale criticism overlooks the power of democratic practices to significantly expand and improve civic connectivity and communication. In the natural wetlands, connectivity often trumps scale. The importance of connectivity is evident in nature in the way cells join to form plants and animals. Think of a coral reef: tiny corals don't get larger; they stick together. In the political wetlands the connections are in public relationships, civic associations, citizen networks, and patterns of public communication.[2] And, since we now live in a more interconnected, global society, "the action of one individual or a small group can affect the whole system very rapidly," observed Carne Ross, based on his experiences as a veteran British diplomat.[3]

Connectivity and Communication

Why are some communities resilient and can bounce back from challenges when others can't? The answer seems to have a lot to do with the nature of the connections that people form with one another and the way information flows.

In *Why the Garden Club Couldn't Save Youngstown*, Sean Safford compares the civic connections in Allentown, Pennsylvania, with those in Youngstown, Ohio.[4] Both cities had been successful manufacturing centers until they experienced similar economic reversals in the late 1970s and early 1980s. Allentown responded better. Why? The way communications flowed appears to have been a factor. Communications that connect disparate parts of a community facilitate public learning.

Youngstown had a civic network organized somewhat like a wagon wheel. Communications went to a central point and then back out. Allentown's communications, on the other hand, were organized in multiple nodes, which promoted "interaction—and mobilization— across social, political, and economic divisions."[5] Anyone could get to most anyone else much as anyone can on the Internet.

Democratic practices facilitate Allentown-type communication because they are decentered. That is, there is no central agency coordinating them. And the projects that grow out of the practices are as varied as the groups that create them. Yet the projects are connected through shared purposes, which makes them more likely to be mutually reinforcing. Naming issues to reflect people's concerns fosters deliberative framing and decision making, which, in turn, promotes the identification of untapped resources and complementary public acting.

Having numerous small initiatives that are connected makes for greater community resilience than depending on a single, large, civic monoculture, which is susceptible to systems failure. Imagine what an up-to-scale 500-pound amoeba would do to the swamps!

What about Leadership?

Democratic practices also run up against the widely held belief that change only occurs when a few courageous leaders step forward to take charge and overcome entrenched power. How could just citizens working with citizens change anything? History is full of examples of great leaders who have been agents of change: Susan B. Anthony, Martin Luther King Jr., Abraham Lincoln, George Washington. You can complete the list.

It is impossible to argue that leaders don't have a great influence. Initiative is essential; someone has to step forward. Democratic practices encourage initiative taking. But they also promote *leaderfulness* rather than just developing a few exceptional leaders. Leaderfulness is another characteristic of resilient communities. In practicing the practices, a great many people from every sector of a community or society can step forward. There is a role for everyone. Some suggest a new way of naming an old problem. Some raise questions about trade-offs. Nearly everyone has an opinion about what should be done to solve a problem. Many have resources to offer. Anyone can participate in evaluating the results of civic efforts.

One study comparing a resilient community that was adept at problem solving with a town that wasn't showed that the town not doing as well actually had better leaders, as traditionally understood. These leaders were highly educated, personally successful, and civically responsible. Yet what stood out in the problem-solving community wasn't so much the qualifications of the leaders as their number, the various parts of the community they were from, and, most of all, the way they interacted with other citizens. The problem solving community had 10 times more people providing leadership than communities of comparable size! The town was leader*ful*.[6]

Initiative is critical even in self-rule because nothing happens spontaneously. Communities that are adept at solving their problems are

Source: Bruce Eric Kaplan, The New Yorker Collection, cartoonbank.com

"We need some sort of useless leader."

leaderful communities in that everyone is expected to provide some initiative. Resilient, problem solving communities make leadership everybody's business, not just the business of a few, and they don't equate leadership exclusively with positions of authority.

In leaderful communities, the people who take initiative are distinguished by the way they interact with their fellow citizens. They are door openers rather than gatekeepers; they are good at making connections. Traditional leaders in positions of authority typically control access to money and give or withhold permission for community projects. Door openers, on the other hand, connect people and broaden participation. They look to the citizenry for solutions, not just to an elite of other leaders.[7]

Henrik Ibsen reminded us that "a community is like a ship; everyone ought to be prepared to take the helm."[8] Given the deep-seated, interrelated problems we face—from joblessness to the breakdown of families—a few good leaders won't be enough. Leadership and citizenship need to become synonymous.

MORE PROBLEMS

Of course, there are more problems of democracy than those that have been dealt with so far in this book. Another glaring problem is the mutual distrust between citizens and major institutions. One of the reasons for using the ecology analogy is that it draws attention to the importance of the relationship between the political wetlands and what happens on dry ground. What is troubling in this relationship is the subject of the next two chapters. However, there isn't just one practice that responds to this problem. Overcoming the distrust and lack of confidence that burdens the relationship requires a better alignment of what institutions do with all the practices citizens use to do what they do. Citizen politics and institutional politics are different, yet they need to be mutually reinforcing.

PART III
INSTITUTIONS, PROFESSIONALS, AND THE PUBLIC

11
BRIDGING THE GREAT DIVIDE

THE GULF SEPARATING PEOPLE from most of our major institutions has been growing for some time and is now enormous. For most institutions, less than half of our citizenry have a great deal of confidence in them.[1]

Comparatively, medical institutions have enjoyed the most confidence, yet barely one-third of Americans would give them a vote of high confidence. Congress has been at the bottom of the list for some time; currently only six percent of people trust its membership. Our legislative branch has become less popular than brussels sprouts. Wall Street is nearly as far down at seven percent. Major companies, law firms, and the press ranked low; about one-third of our citizens have said they had hardly any confidence at all in them.[2]

To be sure, over time attitudes change; lows tend to bottom out; a degree of confidence usually returns. Nonetheless, like an eroding gully, this divide between the public and our institutions threatens the legitimacy of agencies that can't function as they should without the public's trust.

Similar fluctuations in confidence levels affect public schools, academic institutions, and nongovernmental organizations. Furthermore, the lack of confidence is often mutual: just as citizens have difficulty trusting institutions, institutions have difficulty trusting citizens. Since the lack of confidence is mutual, the divide expands from both edges.

"Awesome erosion!"

What's causing the rift? Obviously, many forces are at work, perhaps including unrealistic expectations of institutions. People have other explanations. They say they lack confidence because they believe institutions aren't effective in doing their jobs; they aren't solving problems. And the institutions don't appear to be responsive to the people they are supposed to serve.

These criticisms may be connected. When institutions have a productive working relationship with citizens, the institutions are more likely to be seen as responsive. And, as in the case of schools, institutions seen as responsive are more likely to be seen as effective, particularly if citizens are assisting them.[3] In fact, the institutions may actually be more effective because of the benefits they get from the work citizens do with them. I'll say more about that later. First, I want to dig deeper into the nature of the divide.

The sources of the negative perceptions of institutions aren't hard to find. We've all heard horror tales of corrupt politicians, incompetent teachers, indifferent officials, and bungling bureaucrats. Yet many decent and able people become politicians. And most of the professionals who staff our institutions are dedicated and well trained. Why, then, such lack of confidence?

One of these deeper reasons may have to do with citizens themselves, not institutions. People want responsive and effective institutions, but they want more. They want as much control as they can get in their own hands over their future in a dangerous and unpredictable world. Any relationship with institutions that doesn't give them more control, however positive the relationship may be otherwise, probably won't be enough.

> *The citizen can bring our political and governmental*
> *institutions back to life, make them responsive and*
> *accountable, and keep them honest. No one else can.*
>
> —John Gardner[4]

OBSTACLES TO RESTORING CONFIDENCE

Barriers to restoring confidence are formidable. One is in the difference between civic or democratic mindsets and those of professionals. In making this point, I don't want to give the impression that I am criticizing individual professionals. We all appreciate the skills of competent physicians, carpenters, lawyers, engineers, electricians, and other professionals. I am talking about a culture—professionalism—and its implications for democratic politics.

Putting our institutions in the hands of professionals who are not susceptible to political pressure was supposed to result in greater public benefit and approval. That hasn't happened, and the reason may have to do with a culture that assumes only experts can know best in a complex world. This mindset favors a form of technical rationality that takes on added power when coupled, as it usually is, with the legal authority of bureaucratic institutions. The technical rationality I am referring to sees human society as akin to a machine whose malfunctions can be remedied by instrumental means, like a car engine that doesn't run properly and needs a mechanic.

Technical rationality has a long history. In the early 1900s, Max Weber argued that social behavior, like natural phenomena such as the rotation of planets, follows predictable and calculable patterns. Technical rationality could detect these patterns, which could then be changed by effective and efficient means. (Translation: the car mechanic will know what's wrong and how to correct the problem.) According to Weber, the claim to operate rationally is at the core of modern bureaucratic authority. However, critics worry that instrumental means have a way of becoming detached from ends.[5] (Translation: the car owner knows what he or she wants the car to do, but what this mechanic does may give the vehicle a different function, like turning a family sedan into a race car. What the car can do is no longer connected to what the owner wants it to do.) James Scott, for example, has shown how many top-down social engineering projects around the world have started with noble impulses to improve society, but had disastrous unintended consequences.[6] To use another analogy, imagine society is like a very sophisticated computer that inexplicably fails to boot up or begins to download data from a source you know nothing about. When that happens inexplicably, most of us are baffled. To apply this example to politics, from a professional perspective, people like me are hopeless amateurs. That is exactly how citizens were portrayed in an article in *The Economist* that read, "When professionals dominate all complex subjects, from the forecasting of markets to the cataloguing of library books, perhaps it is too much to hope that public policy can ever be the province of the amateur."[7]

Professionalism brings with it a distinctive notion of service. Professionals usually serve by treating various maladies, and those they treat easily become seen as objects. Doctors have patients, lawyers have clients, print journalists have readers. These "objects" (patients, clients, readers) may be thought of as largely passive or, at best, receptive. (After all, patients are supposed to be patient.) From this perspective, it's easy to think of citizens as *objects* of professional treatment in contrast to the democratic concept of citizens as political actors, as agents.

Democracy exists in inescapable conflict with many assumptions of professionalism, a conflict Woodrow Wilson recognized when he was a scholar in public administration. "Bureaucracy can exist," Wilson wrote, "only where the whole service of the state is removed from the common political life of the people, its chiefs as well as its rank and file."[8]

In her study of the Massachusetts welfare system, cited earlier, Martha Derthick located another conflict between professionalism and democracy in what I would call a difference in "priorities."[9] Originally a locally administered system of relief, the Massachusetts system was, at its best, personal, compassionate, and sensitive to differences among people. The original system was gradually replaced, however, by a professional one with different priorities. The old system put a premium on responsiveness and could distinguish between one person's circumstances and those of a neighbor. Local welfare officials knew people's names and treated them as individuals. The new professional system valued uniformity because the old system was prone to favor some people over others. Everyone was to be treated the same in the new system—no favoritism!

Both the original welfare system and the professional one had downsides as well as advantages. The old system could be corrupted and mismanaged; the new one could be insensitive to differences in people's circumstances and so encumbered by rules that it was difficult for people to navigate.

EFFORTS TO REGAIN LEGITIMACY

In the 21st century we live with the triumph of a professionalized society and owe much of our well-being to it. Nonetheless, the conflict between professional and democratic sensibilities persists. Eager to reclaim their legitimacy, most institutions and many professionals, acutely aware of the public's lack of confidence, have made valiant efforts to restore trust. Their strategies are quite similar, even though the institutions and professions are very different.

One of the first and obvious ways for institutions to respond to criticisms has been to pledge strict adherence to professional standards on the assumption that the pledges will reassure people.[10] Many institutions have also tried to restore public trust by making their operations more transparent. And measures to increase citizen participation have boomed; public hearings or town meetings (meetings *in* towns, not *of* towns) have occurred nearly everywhere. Civic engagement projects have become commonplace.

THE ACCOUNTABILITY MOVEMENT: IS IT HELPING?

Perhaps the most common strategy for governmental and nongovernmental institutions to demonstrate that they aren't unresponsive and ineffective is to provide hard data showing when they have produced good results, which is intended to prove they are accountable.[11] These performance measures are based on various benchmarks, such as the standardized test scores of students in secondary and elementary school.[12]

Although supposedly done to restore public confidence, most accountability projects have another purpose. They are defensive measures intended to protect institutions from what their officials consider unwarranted criticisms and intrusions into their work. That's an understandable reaction, although not one likely to restore public confidence.

> A contemporary scholar of public administration, Christopher Pollitt, argues that, "the presumptions . . . that performance measurement promotes *public* account-ability—are rarely born out by the evidence. . . . There is strikingly little evidence that the makers of PI [performance indicators] systems are particularly concerned about their usefulness to legislators and citizens, as opposed to ministers and managers."[13]

Citizens differ with institutional leaders over what are valid indications of accountability, and they differ even more over the meaning of accountability itself. While institutional leaders typically have in mind information, citizens focus on the kind of relationship they have with schools, as well as with governmental and nongovernmental organizations.[14] In the case of public schools, many Americans have not only been critical, but also have had a declining sense of ownership and responsibility. (Sandy ran into this problem when she tried to get support for improving her community's schools.) People don't always find their relationship with schools to be one marked by responsiveness or accountability.

School officials, on the other hand, may think they are models of accountability, citing the voluminous test score data they publish. They believe these performance measures are in line with the public's demand for higher standards. Citizens, however, may appreciate the information on test performance, yet not be persuaded that the schools are doing the job they want them to do. While most people want students held to high expectations, they think that test scores are only one indication of school performance.[15]

Furthermore, some people believe that they—and their communities, not just the schools—should be held accountable for what happens to the next generation. These citizens think that who should be accountable—and for what—needs to be decided by the public.[16] When accountability is institutionally defined, it tends to disenfranchise citizens.

The accountability movement has also taken hold in grantmaking foundations and in nongovernmental organizations (NGOs). Grantmakers may see demonstrations of accountability as a way to forestall any government intrusion. And they usually think they are being accountable when they use measurable results to show the impact of their funding. Then NGOs, in order to win grants, design their programs with these performance measures in mind.

Externally imposed performance measures can also undermine building civic capacity in communities because civic capacity isn't always measurable, even though it can be demonstrated in other ways. Yet as foundation officials explain, their boards of directors required proof of impact. Grant recipients, for their part, complain that the performance measures are often irrelevant and divert time as well as energy away from more important work. However, recipients said they need the money and have to "play the game" to get it.

Why does demonstrating that grants are having a measurable impact conflict with building civic capacity? The difficulty is proving that the grants themselves and not indigenous factors are responsible for any changes that occur in a community. David Ellerman, formerly of the World Bank, has written insightfully on this difficulty: "the more direct effect foundations and aid agencies try to have, the more they crowd-out, suffocate, and falsify any budding inside-out motivation in the people supposedly being helped to help themselves. Instead of fostering self-help, the money-moving machines foster learned disability and aid addiction."[17] In addition, a study the Kettering Foundation did with the Harwood Institute for Public Innovation shows that the pressure to demonstrate accountability with measurable impact has been turning the focus of some grantmakers inward. They tend to concentrate on professionally defined standards and away from the expectations of the citizens and communities they aim to benefit.[18] For communities, perhaps the most problematic of all the unintended consequences of the accountability measures that rely on outside (objective) evaluators to measure outcomes against predetermined goals has been their effect on collective or public learning. As I have said, one of the most telling characteristics of resilient communities with a history of solving problems is the way these communities learn collectively from their efforts. While outside evaluations have merit, they are quite different from the evaluating that goes on in public learning.

The untoward effects of accountability measures have not just fallen on grant recipients; they can also be an impediment to realizing one of the most cherished objectives of philanthropy—fostering innovation. Innovating requires experimenting, yet experimenting can be at odds with having to show successful outcomes in the near term. Promising experiments often fail. As the head of one community institution that had to show measurable results told me candidly, "I don't have permission to fail."

Inventive experiments might fail to produce the definitive outcomes that performance measures impose, and predetermined performance benchmarks could inhibit community organizations from rethinking goals, which might need to change as experience dictates.[19] Rather than following a predetermined path, inventive communities make the road by walking it.

Without a doubt, citizens involved in experimental ventures recognize the need for clarity of purpose. And they want to know if their efforts have had positive effects. However, since externally imposed accountability measures can stifle experimentation, some civic groups have refused to work with outside funders rather than "playing the game." That not only imposes a hardship on the innovative initiatives, but also is problematic for grantmakers who pride themselves on encouraging creativity. They could become less relevant.

A Vicious Cycle

In the worst cases, institutional efforts to demonstrate accountability may actually increase the loss of public confidence. Not only can accountability demonstrations fail to improve public perceptions, but also they may, in fact, deepen the distrust.

Brian Cook found that "an increasingly vicious circle has emerged in which anxiety about control and accountability . . . has led to more extensive, more complex controls, which in turn have increased the bureaucratic distance between administrators and the public they are expected to serve. This distance then raises new worries about control and accountability and brings about the introduction of another layer of controls."[20] Cook laments that these results are the opposite of what the accountability reforms intend.

Feeding Cynicism

Despite its misuses and often-unintended consequences, we all want accountability in our institutions. As Albert Dzur, the author of *Democratic Professionalism*, points out, "there's real value to accountability—meaning, roughly, that our schools, courts, hospitals, etc., are doing what they say they are doing *and what the public has decided they should do* [emphasis added]." However, Dzur fears this isn't happening; in fact, he sees signs that institutions are moving in the opposite direction by developing even more expert and technical processes in hopes of restoring lost public legitimacy or creating better defenses.[21] He calls this movement "super professionalism."

A better professionalism, from a democratic perspective, would have to deal with citizens' main concerns. Americans have strong feelings, not so much about accountability, but about a lack of it. In their most strident mood, people fume over officials who appear to bask selfishly in privileges and to be grossly unfair in the execution of their duties. Many citizens believe those in positions of authority are trying to protect their own institution or professions. Officials are also thought to be guilty of serious ethical lapses, which compounds the impression that they are irresponsible.

Whether citizens are talking about officeholders in government, business, education, or medicine, the perceptions are similar. Again and again, whatever the field, leaders seem to be on a different page than rank-and-file citizens.

Officeholders can badly misjudge the citizenry's reaction to "proof" of accountability. People want to be informed yet feel overwhelmed by what they consider meaningless numbers. Skeptical of metrics, they think they are being manipulated by the way statistics are used.

Cynicism about being manipulated is widespread and can be found outside the United States. An article by Andrew Gilligan in the United Kingdom's *Telegraph* lambasted the irresponsibility that seems evident when government officials use staged exercises in public consultation with "stakeholders" to get the response that officials want. Gilligan saw these consultations as defensive measures to insulate the officials from citizens. The so-called public meetings were a "ruse," he wrote, "a fraud." He said this "nonsultation," as he called it, "was a cynical technique used by governments, local authorities, and some businesses to provide spurious legitimacy or fake PR cover for a pre-determined decision." Nonsultation, Gilligan believed, was "spreading like knotweed through the bureaucracy."[20] I don't know if we have knotweeds in the United States, but we do have the same criticism of manipulation.

What about Responsibility?

Adding to what I said about the public's view of public schools' accountability, it appears that "accountability" is largely an institutional/professional term. People prefer to talk about responsibility. Accountability is said to be what remains when the responsibility has been taken out.[23] While accountability is typically a matter of information to institutional leaders, it is very much a matter of relationships for citizens. People look for a frank, open, morally grounded exchange with officials. And they want the kind of relationships that provide opportunities for public influence.

Citizens with this kind of connection with institutions tend to be more productively engaged with them. John Gaventa and Gregory

Barrett found that in mutually beneficial relationships, people became more knowledgeable and had a greater sense of their own political efficacy. And the institutions were thought to be more responsive and accountable.[24]

ANOTHER POSSIBILITY: BETTER ALIGNMENT

So what would restore public confidence if that requires citizens having a greater ability to shape their future? I have suggested that at least part of the answer could come from a better alignment of the work of citizens with the work of institutions. I'll give more details in the next chapter, but I am talking about what occurs when institutions and citizens work in a complementary, mutually reinforcing fashion. The work citizens do puts control in their hands, and it also benefits institutions. Institutions become more effective as they profit from the work of citizens. And they are likely to become more responsive when they see the benefits from this work. This sort of mutual benefit could be called symbiosis. (Think of the relationship of bees and flowers.) Or recall

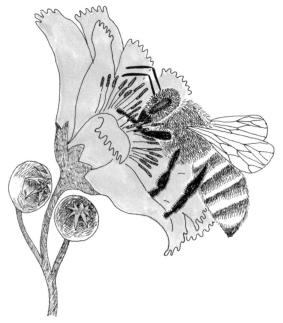

Illustration by Jennifer Berman

the parable of the Blobs and Squares: better alignment would allow the Squares to make greater use of what only the Blobs can produce, and the Blobs would benefit from not being pressured to be more "square."

No More Ships Passing in the Night

All too often, the routines of institutions don't align well with democratic practices because the institutions and citizens aren't on the same page. Institutions want to help; a democratic citizenry wants a stronger hand in shaping the future. So when institutions try to help citizens, their efforts may miss the mark. That was the case on the Gulf Coast, in Bayou La Batre, Alabama, which traces its origins back to an 18th-century French settlement. The residents include Creoles descended from French and West African ancestors, as well as a large group of shrimpers who arrived with their families from Southeast Asia. There had been some disputes among these different groups but, fortunately, no serious clashes. Then, in 2005, the entire community was nearly destroyed by Hurricane Katrina.[25]

The hurricane demolished a good many houses. The fishing industry was also hit hard: boats were blown inland, and it took considerable effort to get them back into the water. Soon after, developers tried to buy a large tract of land in order to build a world-class resort in the village. Some residents saw prosperity just around the corner; others worried that the developers would dominate the reconstruction and shut them out of the decision making about the community's future. People liked to visit Disneyland, but they didn't want to live there. Most of them wanted to restore their community—both its buildings and way of life—and felt that they had to come together as a community to do that.

All the surrounding institutions on the Gulf Coast—charitable organizations, churches, relief agencies—were more than eager to help, and their help was much appreciated. However, relief supplies, grants and loans, and volunteer services didn't speak to the community's most basic question: how can *we* come together to build the kind of community we want? As I've said, that is every community's question regardless of what kind of threat there is.

The Bayou La Batre story is an illustration of what I would call ships passing in the night. The institutions, for the most part, weren't organized to respond to the central question citizens were asking. The institutions had funds and services, but they didn't have much to say about how the community itself might come together to shape its own future, which would mean taking into account the work citizens have to do and the practices they use to do it. Most institutions were focused more on what they could do *for* the community in the near term rather than what they could do *with* the community in the long term. A better alignment would have institutions carrying out their work in ways that made it easier for citizens to do their work—and vice versa.

Reinforcing Democratic Practices

Better alignment between institutions and the citizenry doesn't require massive reform or asking overworked professionals to take on an extra load of new duties. Either would be extremely difficult. Instead, institutional realignment only asks that professionals do what they usually do a bit differently, so that their work reinforces democratic practices.

Alignment is critical because even though leaders of institutions are citizens, the work of citizens and the work of institutions are different, as I've tried to show. Recall that the work of citizens involves people naming problems, framing issues, deciding deliberatively, identifying local resources, acting in a complementary fashion, and learning together. These democratic practices have their counterparts in institutional routines. Institutions—governments, schools, nonprofit organizations—also name, frame, decide, commit resources, coordinate actions, and learn. While the tasks are the same, they are carried out in distinctive ways. Alignment respects those differences; it is an alternative to colonization.

Next, I'll report in detail on experiments or the potential for experiments where institutions have aligned, or could better align their work with that of citizens by taking account of the way the public carries out democratic practices.

12
EXPERIMENTS IN REALIGNMENT AND POSSIBILITIES FOR EXPERIMENTS

SOME INSTITUTIONS AND PROFESSIONALS are already trying to realign their work with the practices citizens use in theirs.[1] Because one of the greatest obstacles to a better alignment is the difference between what institutions think the public needs to know and what citizens consider relevant, I'll start by reporting on experiments where knowledge is central, which is in universities, colleges, secondary schools, and the media. Many of the experiments cited are variations of projects that are quite commonplace. What is distinctive about them is the control they put in citizens' hands and how they bridge the divide separating the public from institutions.

What's the incentive for institutions to undertake experiments that put more control in people's hands? Even if the experiments don't take power away from institutions, how does realignment serve their self-interest, which is to be effective in their job? The answer, I believe, is the reinforcement that can come from the complementary work of citizens.

Some of the examples of realignment I am about to give are still not fully developed. I cite them to show their potential to strengthen the hands of citizens as well as to bolster the work of institutions. Like a meteorologist forecasting the weather, I'll describe conditions that seem likely to bring about a change—in this case, that are likely to produce realignment. I won't be reporting only on experiments that have already been done but also on the potential for experimentation, beginning with journalism.[2]

IN JOURNALISM

Cole Campbell, a former newspaper editor and dean of the school of journalism at the University of Nevada, went beyond the truism that the press informs the public to ask exactly what kind of information people need to govern themselves.[3] The standard answer has been "the facts." Cole was beginning to challenge that answer when he died tragically in an automobile accident. Other journalists were also exploring questions similar to the one that Cole asked in their evolving understanding of their role. What if journalists saw their audience as more than just readers and viewers? What if they thought of readers and viewers as citizens?[4] What would this mean for the way they go about their work?

Cole's question about what citizens need to know becomes sharper when put in the context of an argument made by Davis "Buzz" Merritt, a newspaper editor in Wichita, Kansas, who insisted that the problems of his community weren't going to be solved unless the citizens did the work they needed to do with other citizens.[5] As he explained, "We have to view citizens not as an audience—as readers or nonreaders—but as a public, as potential actors."[6] In that context, Cole's question could be rewritten as, what do our readers need to know in order to *do the work* involved in solving common problems?

Cole began to see that "just facts" weren't enough to inform the public while editor of the *Virginian-Pilot* in Norfolk. To find out what the citizenry was thinking, he sent reporters to people's homes where there were small forums of friends and neighbors. In those settings, the journalists were able to hear how people described their problems in terms meaningful to them; they didn't cite facts as much as personal experiences. Then Cole used what the reporters heard to pose questions to candidates in an upcoming election. The experiment showed that the names the candidates had for problems weren't at all the same as the ones citizens used.

This experiment is particularly significant because Cole didn't use focus groups or a demographically correct public to get at the public's concerns. He operated on the assumption that no one can truly represent our individual voice, however much they may look like us. And his experiment assumed that people form their opinions with those they normally talk to in their families, neighborhoods, and workplaces.

More experiments in journalism like Cole's could be stimulated by using an insight from Dan Yankelovich to frame issues in public terms. Dan refers to what Kettering calls the "names of problems" as "points of departure." He uses the issue of freedom of expression to illustrate the difference between professional points of departure and those of citizens.[7] Professional journalists define freedom of the press in a way that reflects what is most important to them as producers of speech: they interpret the First Amendment as giving them the right to *say* whatever they think needs to be said. Alarmed when polls show that people can't distinguish the First from the other amendments, journalists may conclude that the public is ignorant or doesn't consider free speech important. What they miss is the way Americans actually think about the First Amendment. Citizens do believe in it; yet their point of departure is their need for information. The public believes that the First Amendment ensures the right to *hear*, to have free access to all sides of an issue, not just the right to speak.

Experiments like Cole's don't require journalists to take on new roles because they already name problems and frame issues.[8] They only have to take into account the names and frameworks that are useful in civic work. The payoff for journalists? The citizenry is more likely to get civically involved if journalists name problems to reflect what people consider valuable. Involved citizens make good subscribers.

An experiment in aligning the media's framework for decision making with a public framing occurred in Springfield, Missouri, on an issue of juvenile crime. It suggests that the public welcomes such experiments. The local newspaper laid out a range of options for combating the crime problem, not the usual two, which prompted deliberative decision making in the community. However, on the next issue, one involving school finance, the paper returned to the conventional, bipolar framing. That made a difficult decision even more difficult; there weren't enough deliberations to give citizens a better understanding of all their options or the pros and cons of each. People in Springfield complained to the newspaper's editor. Clearly, the paper knew how to be helpful on the first issue, why did it revert to form on the second?[9]

In other communities, the media has experimented with aligning their coverage of issues with a framework intended to reinforce public deliberation. In State College, Pennsylvania, the *Centre Daily Times* collaborated with a local group sponsoring NIF forums.[10] The newspaper printed a deliberative framework on its editorial page and then reported on the community forums that used the framework. And in Philadelphia, broadcast journalists, local foundations, and the University of Pennsylvania have collaborated on projects that prompted public deliberation on controversial issues like reductions in the city budget. One objective of the Philadelphia projects was to find out how citizens weighed the difficult choices that have to be made in budgeting.[11]

I believe other experiments to more closely align the communication of news to public ways of knowing could occur in new media. Sometimes called "citizen media" to distinguish it from professional journalism, the people "formerly known as the audience" are reaching other people in remarkable ways.[12] But for realignment to occur, new media will have to provide the kind of interpersonal interaction that motivates people to take in the experience of others. That is key to the social construction of practical wisdom, where speaking is not as important as listening.

IN ACADEME

Colleges and universities are wellsprings of the knowledge that is constructed through rigorously disciplined scientific inquiry. Academics sometimes make a distinction between this knowledge, which they call "objective," and what they consider subjective, idiosyncratic knowledge, or opinion, which can vary from individual to individual. I would refer back to what I said earlier about how this distinction underestimates the value of the way citizens create knowledge or practical wisdom.[13] Publicly constructed knowledge is sometimes dismissed as just opinions without the benefit of facts, ignoring the rich literature on moral reasoning that makes use of the human faculty for judgment.[14]

Redefining Scholarship

Many of the experiments in the academy have had to do with aligning scientifically constructed knowledge with socially or publicly constructed knowledge. These experiments are occurring in a new field called "public scholarship," a field that has emerged because some faculty members want to do more than just provide expert advice. They haven't rejected their own expertise by any means, yet they have seen its limits.

Professor Alejandro Sanz de Santamaría is a prime example of a public scholar. His research was on the economic development of rural communities in Colombia. Surveying the literature on these communities, he found extensive data on the characteristics of the soil, on weather conditions, and on the growth rate of the population. Yet when he did his fieldwork, he realized that the data he was using didn't fit the complexities of the social conditions in rural communities. Most disconcerting of all, he saw that his way of producing knowledge wasn't like the way villagers created knowledge. Alejandro's discomfort led him to change both the way he did research and the way he taught research in the classroom. He abandoned the assumption that the villages were "broken" and his job was to fix them. I would say that he moved from "replace what grows" politics to "build on what grows" politics. And he set out to find ways to communicate what he had learned as an economist that were consistent with the way people learned.[15]

Other experiments in public scholarship have occurred in academic fields like community development and community health. They are also going on in cooperative extension, out of concern for rural communities.[16] At Penn State, Ted Alter makes a strong case for broadening the definition of research to make room for experiments in realignment. Scott Peters at Syracuse has used his research to capture stories of numerous academics doing publicly relevant studies. And Frank Fear at Michigan State has pushed the boundaries of the university engagement movement by challenging academe's concept of the role of citizens. (A complete list of scholars doing experiments in aligning scholarly knowledge with publicly created knowledge would go beyond the scope of this book.[17])

In other cases, an entire university, not just a few faculty members, has recognized the importance of public scholarship. The Suggsville example was based, in large part, on an experiment in public scholarship at Auburn University.[18]

Auburn's realignment experiment began when support for a technical assistance project collapsed as a result of the election of a new mayor. The previous mayor had been Auburn's ally, but his successor wanted his own project, so Auburn had to change from being an expert adviser to a new role, which involved encouraging what I've called democratic practices. On the surface, Auburn's interventions were sometimes nothing more than placing the meeting room chairs in a circle rather than rows. (In Suggsville this prevented people from one part of the community from congregating on the back seats while those from other sections dominated the first rows.) Beneath the surface, Auburn was developing a different way to engage the community that went beyond service.

Concentrating on the Role of Citizens

Still other experiments in realignment have come from new centers for public or civic life in community colleges, state colleges, liberal arts colleges, and universities. What makes these experiments distinctive is their attention to the role of citizens.[19] A number of the centers focus on the practice of public deliberation and help communities to name and frame issues in ways that promote the careful weighing of options and avoid polarization. The kind of issues they frame have had the potential to be quite disruptive—redrawing electoral district lines, building near fragile coastal islands, preventing teenage pregnancies.

The campus centers differ widely in structure and purpose, yet they have common roots. They were created primarily by public scholars, although several were the initiative of civic entrepreneurs who found allies on campus. Some centers have their own boards, involve more than one institution, and have nonprofit status.[20] Others draw their support from institutional budgets. And while independent from Kettering, many have an ongoing relationship with the foundation that is based on joint research.

The number of centers has grown significantly over two decades. Part of this growth may be in response to citizens' concerns about the lack of a common or public voice in the political system and part in response to requests from nearby communities to help solve problems.

Within academe, centers are finding partners in a number of fields. Political scientists have become interested in deliberative democracy, philosophers have taken up deliberative theory, and scholars in communication studies have delved into the tradition of rhetoric to revive moral reasoning and practical wisdom. In addition, major academic divisions such as cooperative extension have begun rediscovering their democratic roots and reexamining their relationship to communities as the number of farmers needing technical assistance continues to decline.

If ships aren't to pass in the night, academic centers are in an ideal position to engage communities in conversations about how they can come together to solve their problems. Problem solving is work, and many of the centers have a good sense of how this work is done.

Some of the centers also collaborate with secondary and elementary schoolteachers who are introducing deliberative decision making into the curriculum. That is direct alignment of a democratic practice with what happens in schools. These civic education experiments have been going on at centers such as the ones at Hofstra University, the Wisconsin Institute for Public Policy and Services, and the Center for Civic Life in Alabama, to give three examples. Several of the centers hold institutes for teachers and involve colleges of education to reach new teachers.[21]

The Alabama center has been working with the state department of education, the state social studies council, and teacher preparation courses in colleges of education in its summer institute. Hofstra has instituted a course of deliberative politics for students seeking teaching certificates. And the Wisconsin Institute has reached out to potential high school dropouts in its program of deliberative pedagogy and has involved a local school board.[22] Similar efforts are being made at Miles College in Alabama and at the University of Northern Iowa.

Introducing College Students to a Politics They Can Use

I've been particularly impressed by the potential in involving undergraduates in realigning the work of academic institutions with the work of citizens. The realignment begins by introducing students to the problem solving work that citizens do with citizens. On some campuses, students have been introduced to deliberative decision making, both in experiments by centers and in faculty initiatives. In more direct realignment, faculty members have used the NIF issue books to introduce deliberative politics in classes ranging from drama to law. One of the most elaborate experiments involving deliberative decision making was done at Wake Forest over a full undergraduate cycle of four years; the results are described in detail in *Speaking of Politics* by Professors Katy Harriger and Jill McMillan.[23]

Briefly, the Wake Forest experiment introduced a group of students to deliberative politics at multiple sites: in classrooms, on campus, and in the town where the university is located. Deliberating was not presented as just a way of conducting forums but as a way of living democratically. Harriger and McMillan also found that the concept of politics implicit in deliberations calls into question all the roles professors have become accustomed to as teachers, researchers, and even citizens. (Alejandro Sanz de Santamaría made a similar discovery about the way what happens off campus carries over to the campus.)

One part of the Wake Forest experiment that deserves special attention is the impact on the students who participated, which was profound. One participant said that it affected everything she did in her activities with other students and even in her personal relationships. Politics, the students discovered, involves more than electing representatives. Understanding that gave them an expanded sense of the many ways they could be effective political actors.[24]

Experiments on other campuses are underway to give students direct experience in the full range of community problem solving by embedding them in towns and cities where they can learn about the work of citizens. Students "enroll" in community just as they enroll in the academic department where they major. The faculty want students to be around long enough to experience the consequences of what they do. Opportunities for students to be involved in service projects already abound, and while these are useful, they don't necessarily give students experiences in collective decision making and action on community-defined problems. Faculty members leading these experiments say their goal is to develop a program that will provide both curricular and community-based opportunities for undergraduates to learn what it is like to solve problems with people from diverse backgrounds and with varied interests.[25]

IN PUBLIC EDUCATION

Our public school system, which suffers from a particularly viru-
lent case of declining confidence, could surely benefit from a closer
alignment with the work citizens do to educate. As the public's sense
of ownership of and responsibility for the schools has declined, the
schools have responded by improving two-way communications with
parents as well as by developing an array of public engagement initiatives. Yet the loss of ownership and responsibility persists, as does the
lack of confidence.

From Public Relations to Public Relating

Before describing the experiments to realign what schools do with
the work of citizens, I want to say more about the effect of engagement efforts to improve the relationship between the public and its
schools. Critics of these efforts argue that they are not citizen-led and
haven't affected the fundamental relationship between communities
and schools.[26] Certainly the engagement efforts are still evolving. I
think there are more possibilities for crossing the divide that separates
the public from the public schools, if this evolution continues. In particular, I think there are ways engagement efforts can be better aligned
with people's desire to get more control over the future.

As discussed in the last chapter, the other standard strategy schools
have used to rebuild confidence has been to offer evidence of accountability. While this strategy has limitations, there have been efforts to
improve it. For instance, some professionals in school public relations
have recognized that engagement has to go beyond creating a better
image for schools.[27] Perceptive professional groups like the National
School Public Relations Association (NSPRA) have encouraged
schools to move from public relations to "public relating." Following
that advice might open the door to experiments in realignment.

This door could open even wider if the impetus came from the
public. The Southwest Educational Development Laboratory (SEDL)
found neighborhood-based organizations that had reached beyond

the schools to the communities where they were located.[28] These initiatives were markedly unlike typical school engagement efforts because they were led by parents and community members with a broad educational agenda. Such initiatives might offer opportunities for new experiments in realignment.

Other community-led initiatives—particularly in low-income neighborhoods—have been neither antagonistic toward school officials nor aimed at reducing their power. Rather they have attempted to change "the adversarial relationships that too often exist between schools and the wider community."[29] The strategy has been to strengthen the public's ability to act and then to use that ability to work on problems in education.[30] That strategy serves both the schools and democracy.

After studying these community initiatives, Clarence Stone characterized them as having "less to do with challenging the control mechanisms of established elites than with the character of the conditions necessary for viable relationships." Stone found that, while citizens used adversarial methods extensively in the 1960s and 1970s, the effects were limited. He saw a potential for a shift to building civic capacity for solving problems in education.[31] A focus on community capacity building, whenever and wherever it occurs, could create opportunities for realignment with schools because many of the schools' problems have to be solved in and by communities.

Using All That Educates

Some citizens, frustrated with the schools, have begun educational projects they describe as "doing what the schools don't." I'm not talking about home schooling or charter schools, but experiments to use community resources to educate and address problems that schools can't hope to address alone.

Those using local resources to educate have been called "community educators"; they find educational resources in the community that can supplement what the schools have.[32] Communities already educate through libraries, museums, community centers, and places of worship. But community educators draw on what may seem unlikely resources such as the old cemetery used to teach history in Lexington. These educators include local artists, business leaders, economic development professionals, police, firefighters, and naturalists. Community educators say their work is mentoring, building character, and developing cultural identity.

The need for an alignment between the work of community educators and the schools is obvious. The more the schools reinforce the work of citizens in employing community resources to educate, the better off the schools are. And the more the work of citizens improves the schools, the better off the community is.

Typically, community educators don't think they can or should teach, at least not in the way teachers do. Still, they believe they can educate. In this context, when people talk about teaching, they mean instruction in a subject; "educating" means helping young people develop a faculty for learning. A good example is the project I cited that involved churches where citizens came to see their own power to educate when they looked at what they had learned to do well and where they had learned it. These people realized that even though they hadn't taught as schools do, they had, nonetheless, educated.

Marion Brady, a retired teacher and school administrator, defines education as helping "students make more sense of the world, themselves, and others." This is very much like what citizens describe as their objective in using community resources to educate.[33]

Once again, the challenge of alignment is to mesh the instruction that goes on in the classroom with the work of educating that goes on outside.

Focusing on Citizenship

Probably the greatest opportunity for realignment between the work of citizens and the work of schools is in preparing young people to be citizens. The community—including parents, religious organizations, and youth clubs—has the greatest influence on how young people come to see their role as citizens. When in league with the civic work of communities, schools cannot only support community efforts, they can use what communities do to enrich their own civics courses.

Civics has, regrettably, lost some of its original focus on citizens. In the nation's formative years, nearly all education had civic purpose.[34] The earliest common schools were created to serve public rather than narrow pedagogical purposes. They were to complete the great work of the Revolution—to produce citizens capable of turning the dream of a new republic into a reality. Then, in the post-Revolutionary era of national growth, civic education took on new purposes. Popular schooling was to create one nation out of diverse groups with long histories of destructive conflicts in Europe. Civic education was an education in what Americans shared and what was distinctive about the emerging national culture.

In the 19th century, civic education occurred in a great many institutions and took a variety of forms: Fourth of July oratory, patriotic poems, songs, parades, works of art, biographies of exemplary Americans, histories of the new country. Civic education was a public enterprise. And it was about citizens, as well as governments. Social responsibility was emphasized. To be sure, young people in the 19th century were exposed to a highly partisan, sometimes physically combative, politics. And many of the cultural events that educated are still with us. The point here isn't to glorify the 19th century. The point is that civic education today is largely about the relationship of citizens to the state rather than the relationship of citizens to citizens as well as to the state.

By the early 20th century, our political environment had changed— and so had our concept of civic education. We placed a great deal of confidence in a science with facts to be mastered, a science with universal principles to be understood. Politics was recast as political science and civic education became largely a study of how government works. (You may remember the "Schoolhouse Rock!" lesson on how a bill is passed.) The notion that all education is civic education was gradually replaced by the idea that we had to have specialized courses in the science of politics, and, more narrowly, the science of government. Science was a subject for classrooms, not communities.

By the beginning of the 21st century, educators and civic leaders were speaking out in alarm about what they believed was a decline in civic education.[35] And some who were outspoken called not simply for a revival of civics focused on history and government but a new civics with citizens at the center—citizens who were political actors, not just volunteers in good causes.

This trend creates opportunities for classrooms to break new ground if what teachers teach can be aligned with the work of citizens joining forces with other citizens. Experience in that work should develop active, enterprising young citizens who know how to solve problems with others. And the people they work with in a community should be ideal instructors if joined by classroom teachers who provide relevant lessons from history, political science, and other subjects.

Experiments are already underway that give students experiences in collective decision making to solve common problems. Auburn University students are spending their summers in towns across Alabama as part of a civic-engagement program called Living Democracy.[36] Secondary schools are also giving students opportunities in deliberative decision making. In Birmingham, AL, middle and high school students have deliberated on curbing youth violence. Schools on Long Island as well as in Wausau, WI, and State College, PA, are also experimenting with using deliberation in the classroom.[37]

Reframing School Issues as Community Issues

Realignment has to serve the self-interest of institutions. And I believe the potential for that to occur may be greater now because of greater recognition that the "schools cannot do it alone."[38] In that same vein, it is quite apparent that schools alone can't overcome all the outside problems that interfere with learning and spill over into the classroom. Schools need the reinforcement of civic work in combating these difficulties. So, they have a stake in strengthening their community's capacity to do civic work.[39]

A school district in Pueblo, Colorado, experimented with reframing a school problem as a community issue. They received a large grant to promote health education, which would have added a course on sex education to the curriculum. A dispute over the course soon threatened to polarize the community. The schools were caught in the middle between opposing factions. Because the controversy couldn't be resolved, the grant was revoked. Losing the money only intensified the dispute.[40]

With the help of the Colorado Association of School Boards, Pueblo began a series of community naming exercises to find out exactly what was troubling people. Surprisingly, given the controversy, the meetings showed that most people weren't as concerned about sex education in the schools as they were about teenage pregnancy in the community. That issue had been masked by the debate over sex education. Using the results from the school board's town meetings, citizens in Pueblo then renamed and reframed the issue. The changes they made were instrumental in creating an initiative to enlist a number of community agencies in helping reduce teenage pregnancies.

Renaming issues so that communities recognize and accept their responsibilities should be particularly helpful to classroom teachers. Teachers are often frustrated by what happens (or doesn't happen) in the community. They are buffeted by a world of social problems that fester outside the classrooms and eventually find their way inside. The effects of these problems can be devastating when they affect student behavior. I remember a teacher in Houston, Texas, telling me, "I spend 60 percent of my time on discipline, 20 percent on filing, and, if I am lucky, I have 20 percent left for instruction." School personnel say they have to shoulder more and more of the immense responsibility of raising children, even to the point of feeding and supervising them after school.[41]

When a problem is recognized as the community's and not the school's alone, the response can be quite different than when it isn't. A lawyer who served on his local school board complained about the poor attendance at public meetings on school discipline. Later, when he became a district attorney, he noticed that town meetings on juvenile crime drew overflow crowds. Despite some differences, school discipline and juvenile crime are related issues. So why were people so much more attentive to one than to the other? Perhaps because of differences in the way the problems were named. The very name "discipline" suggests that the problem is one that the schools should handle. Consequently, only a few citizens felt obligated to do anything beyond finding out what the educators were doing. But, when antisocial behavior spreads to the streets and into people's homes, it becomes everyone's problem.

Recognizing the community issues that affect schools can promote community mobilization for education, and that mobilization can strengthen democratic practices, build stronger public relationships, and reinforce norms of cooperation. Robert Putnam's research shows a powerful correlation between school outcomes and civic norms and relationships.[42] (I would add democratic practices to norms and relationships.) The research is clear: school performance is materially affected by the work citizens do.

OVERCOMING BARRIERS TO REALIGNMENT

Despite the advantages, school-community realignment is difficult for several reasons. From a school's perspective, the resources of a community don't look at all like the resources professionals use. Furthermore, the work of citizens using community resources to educate doesn't mesh easily with the way schooling is organized. What students learn in communities doesn't always fit in the curriculum nor can it be evaluated by standardized tests. Adding to the barriers to alignment, a professional code says teaching requires an expertise that citizens don't have. And the community may be seen as a liability, not a resource. As one educator of 25 years confessed, "I was trained to counter influences from outside my classroom, not to work with the public."

There have been, however, alignment experiments that do connect classrooms to the civic work of community educators. Remember the Kentucky horse farm; an alternative school was also involved. Nearly everybody in the area (Lexington) loves horse racing. And some of these horse-lovers were distressed when they found that, after the winners of the Kentucky Derby had passed their prime, they went to the glue factory. So they started buying these old champions and putting them out on a farm they named "Old Friends." Then, at the invitation of the farm, the principal of the alternative school began sending students to work with the horses. Along with the work, the school added a little instruction. Zoology probably wasn't so formidable in the context of racehorses. Kids who had no interest in the classrooms were beginning to learn.[43]

Other communities have recognized that many local institutions educate, not just horse farms. In Chattanooga, a civic group identified the many places where young people learned something useful and drew a map of all its educating institutions, including but not confined to schools.[44]

Reversing the Equation: Seeing the Community Itself as an Educating Institution

One of the greatest barriers to realigning the work of schools with civic work in the communities may be that the equation being used is backwards. The assumption is that the school is the primary educator and the community is to play a supporting role. But what if that is wrong? What would happen if we thought of the community as the principal educator and saw the school in a supporting role? Realignment would mean adapting what the schools do to mesh with the educating that a community does.

Seeing the community as the primary educator also has obvious implications for the way communities are understood. It suggests that communities aren't just places to live or to work. They exist to do more than provide services and protect the physical well-being of residents.

Communities are responsible for providing people with opportunities to develop to their fullest potential. And that requires them to educate.

One of the boldest arguments for seeing the community as the primary educating institution is in the work of Edmund Gordon, professor emeritus at Columbia's Teachers College.[45] He makes a strong case for concentrating on communities rather than on schools, apart from communities. Sandy, the teacher turned capacity builder who I described in the beginning of the book, is following Gordon's advice in focusing on the community in an effort to strengthen schools. What would this reverse realignment look like? A possibility: One way communities educate is to give people direct, personal experiences in what democratic citizens do. Juries, municipal governing bodies, and school boards are democracy's workshops. So are town meetings and public forums. They all "teach" the practices of deciding and acting together on difficult issues. Rather than just watching what adults do, teachers can give their students experiences in grappling with these same issues in forums with adults. (Senior citizen centers have already been sites for some of this civic education.)

Gordon's argument for seeing the community as the primary educator resonates with the research of Larry Cremin, who documented the educational role communities have always played in America. Cremin, a Pulitzer Prize–winning historian, identified a variety of educating institutions other than schools in his three-volume comparative history of education in America. He showed that the country has long educated through families, along with faith-based institutions, libraries, museums, benevolent societies, youth groups, agricultural fairs, radio and television stations, newspapers, and military organizations.[46]

Given this history, it seems reasonable to ask why communities don't connect their educating institutions to take advantage of all the resources that could be used to promote learning. Certainly schools have field trips to zoos, museums, and the like. And many upper-middle-class communities are bursting with after-school enrichment programs and summer activities. These, however, are only a fraction of the local institutions and activities with the potential to educate.

Cremin also pointed out the anomaly of having boards of *education* that select only superintendents for *schools*. He wasn't suggesting that school boards actually take control of libraries, museums, and other educating institutions. He was simply encouraging people to imagine what might happen if communities broadened their focus from schooling to educating.

Conceivably, communities might build a network linking all of their educating Squares and Blobs. Such a network might create a strategy for comprehensive educational development, somewhat like those strategies that are routinely devised for economic development, but that possibility has yet to be explored.

Is coalescing all educating institutions simply a matter of coordination, one that could be addressed by chartering a new central agency to connect all the players into a system? I think not. The best response to the challenge might be for all the educating agencies to concentrate on enriching the culture of learning in the community. Research shows that some cultures promote education much more than others and what this culture supports has everything to do with what happens in schools and beyond.[47]

Strengthening the Culture of Learning

Little would bring down barriers to realignment as much as broadening the focus of efforts to reunite the public and the public schools to take into account a community's culture of learning. Communities educate most powerfully through the norms and social expectations that influence the way people regard learning; that is, the importance they place on it and the kind of learning they prize. A culture of learning is reflected in the work citizens do with citizens. An example: in one community, citizens said that everyone in the town was trying to educate the next generation.[48] That may have been a bit of an overstatement, but businesses had internships; churches had after-school programs; civic organizations sponsored sports teams. They all did what they did because the community expected it of them. And the responsibility people felt for education was more significant than any of their programs. In other words, what was being done (which was actually very common) wasn't as significant as the culture that reinforced the expectations.

A neighborhood in St. Paul, Minnesota, had an explicit cultural strategy. People tapped neighborhood resources to educate by drawing on local history. Mary Boyd, who was in the forefront of this work, believed that cultural knowledge and identity raised the confidence of young people and encouraged them to take an active, positive role in their community.[49] St. Louis Park, Minnesota, and Albion, Michigan, have also had communitywide initiatives to strengthen cultures of learning. In these cases, the objective was to set a precedent for local organizations to take responsibility for educating young citizens. In St. Louis Park, community organizations made a covenant to put children first. In Albion, these organizations enlisted citizens from all across the community to do whatever they could to make a constructive difference in the lives of young people. What they did was conventional: tutoring, mentoring, and the like. Why they did it, to change the culture, as a strategy for community development, was novel.[50]

What would be evidence of a rich culture of learning? There would be more community educators and more restaurants teaching the languages of their cuisine, more churches and civic organizations helping people to recognize their power to educate, more businesses offering internships.

It might seem that school boards, whose members come from the community, would be leading in strengthening the culture of learning and in using all of the community's local educating institutions. Boards could represent the community to the school (rather than just representing the school to the community). Regrettably, that doesn't appear to happen very often. And it may not be entirely the fault of board members. School boards face almost insurmountable obstacles if they were to try to play a broader role. The enormous burden of rules and regulations that constrain these boards can prevent them from adding more duties to their already overloaded agendas. And other community institutions may not accept school boards as neutral conveners.

The impetus for realignment probably has to come from elsewhere in a community, ideally with the support of school boards.

IN NONGOVERNMENTAL
ORGANIZATIONS (NGOS)

Aligning civic work with the work of nongovernmental organizations should be easy; after all, these are civic organizations. The NGOs are nonprofits that include large national civic organizations, local community organizations, and grantmaking foundations. They aren't all alike by any means, and when I report on the experiments in realignment, the findings will not be applicable in all cases. Although not plagued with as great a loss of confidence as other institutions, many NGOs have problems with their own legitimacy as agents of the citizenry. People don't always think nongovernmental organizations are any different from governmental ones. They appear to be more like Squares than Blobs.

As organizations in the nongovernmental or independent sector have become larger and more professional—and as they have become deputized by government agencies to provide social services and take over other government roles—NGOs have become more like the organizations in government. Some have also been colonized by governments; that is, they have aligned their routines with bureaucratic routines, not democratic practices. In their defense, because they are funded with tax dollars, they have to show that they have made good use of the funds. That is why many NGOs, like grantmakers, have turned to "scientific" or measurable standards, using quantitative benchmarks, to prove they have done a good job.

However, those civic organizations that usually depend on grants, have found the pressure to show measureable results—and quickly— can be counterproductive. Their accomplishments are often intangible and slow to develop. As Bruce Sievers, an experienced leader in philanthropy, has pointed out, there are also fallacies or blind spots in the prevailing epistemological assumptions—primarily the assumption that there is expert knowledge that can lead to effective social and political controls.[51] (Bruce is another who argues for greater appreciation of practical knowledge.) Greater appreciation would be an inducement to experiment with realignments to take advantage of knowledge that citizens produce by deliberating.

Starting Small/Staying Small

Despite pressures that come from the fixation on quantitative measures, which are used as indications of "getting up to scale," some civic organizations and their foundation allies are marching to a different drummer. They have the potential to do experiments in alignments by supporting the work of citizens that starts small and stays small.[52]

These nongovernmental organizations include place-based foundations that see the value in projects that give citizens a greater ability to chart their own course. Many are local foundations interested in how citizens come together to strengthen communities and the roles that grantmakers can play other than just financial.[53] For example, one of these foundations "funds" new civic organizations by connecting them with networks of potential allies.

Realignment in NGOs could also be strengthened by collaborating with experiments going on in other sectors. For instance, community foundations may find fellow travelers in cooperative extension divisions that are turning their attention to building the civic capacities of communities. And these two groups may find they have much in common with governmental organizations that try to function more like citizen-centered NGOs. These government agencies aren't just regulating communities; they are trying to rejuvenate them. In West Virginia's coal country, the US Department of the Interior has partnered with Volunteers in Service to America (VISTA) to assist community groups in cleaning up the environment.[54] When the professionals in government depend on citizens acting, they are likely to encounter the practices citizens use to do their work. And that could provide opportunities to align professional routines with democratic practices. It will take more experiments to see what realignment would look like, but the potential is there.

NGO experiments in realignment can learn from a 1990s philanthropic initiative called "civil investing."[55] The initiative was a response to a growing realization that grants weren't effective, not because of a lack of performance standards, but because of a lack of civic capacity in the communities receiving the grants. The lesson learned was that grantmakers have to make investments in community building.

Community building is still an objective for some foundations, and investing in it gives them an opportunity to see the practices that make communities work (that is, the practices that enable communities to solve their problems). This insight has the potential to prompt a reconsideration of foundation routines that may disrupt the practices that are essential to citizen-centered democracy. This potential was evident in a conversation among foundations about civil investing that began with them talking about what they thought democracy meant. One answer was self-determination. With that definition in mind, someone suggested looking at how their foundations decided on grant programs. Their usual practice, these grantmakers said, was to select a problem, name it, get expert advice on how to solve it, and then develop a funding program. The expert advice was translated into criteria for getting grants and specifications for the outcomes to be achieved. At this point someone asked, "Is what we are doing really promoting self-determination?" That question alone doesn't bring about realignment, but it is the first step toward it.

My point is that better alignment requires looking into the routines of grantmakers, not just the grants themselves. This kind of introspection challenges deeply ingrained institutional mindsets and protocols. An official from a large NGO that distributes millions for community development observed that one of the first obstacles to realignment was altering the grantmaker–grant recipient relationship. If that relationship is based on the assumption that the NGO is the incarnation of democratic civil society with all of its virtues, the assumption can lead to an all-too-comfortable operational pattern. The grantmaker claims a moral high ground because it acts on behalf of ordinary citizens. But operationally, it doesn't necessarily go through the considerable trouble of actually working with people.

NGOs have powerful incentives to keep their relationships with communities much as they are. Rather than building civic capacity, a relationship of mutual dependency develops in which grantmakers remain in the confines of their role as benefactors providing money, services, or both. Grassroots organizations then position themselves in relation to those funders where they are most likely to get support, or they develop programs they think funders want. Consequently, grantmakers have little incentive to build a greater capacity in communities for self-sustaining projects. And grant recipients, rather than developing their capacity to invent their own future, concentrate on skills like grant writing.

IN GOVERNMENT

For if liberty and equality, as is thought by some, are chiefly to be found in democracy, they will be best attained when all persons alike share in the government to the utmost.

—Aristotle[56]

Shifting the spotlight from nongovernmental organizations to governmental ones doesn't change the picture very much. Think back to the problem of the divide separating the public from the government and people's lack of confidence even in their elected representatives. Arguably, a better alignment with democratic practices could improve the troubled relationships with institutions of government in ways that would strengthen democratic self-rule. And reinforcement from the work of democratic citizens would serve governments' self-interest in greater effectiveness.

The "citizenship gap"—that dead-air space, so to speak,
that vacuum—between the people and their government . . .
is a greater threat to our government and our social
structure than any external threat by far.
                                        —Hubert Humphrey[57]

The Legislative Branch

What might this realignment look like with national, state, and local assemblies? Some experiments have attempted to bring the work that citizens do in deliberation to bear on legislative policymaking, not as a special interest group would to change a policy, but to change the relationship between the public and legislative bodies. Public deliberation—which enhances people's ability to make sound decisions and to speak in a shared, reflective, or public voice—could provide officeholders with information about how to engage the citizenry on its own terms—and in the process, help combat the hyperpolarization that is jamming the political system. Although the outcomes of public deliberations don't tell legislators how to vote, they can provide insights into strategies for involving the public before representatives say "yea" or "nay."

In 2008, deliberative forums on the health care issue showed that citizens had not "fully explore[d] the reasons why health-care costs are rising," and they had not worked through the trade-offs among policy options. The implication for engaging the public was that the citizenry was likely to be polarized if there weren't more opportunities to identify costs and consequences and work through the tensions.[58] And that is what happened. Could more public deliberation have prevented the polarization? Perhaps not. Could it have lessened the severity of the polarization? Perhaps so.

The greatest potential for realigning government routines with the work of citizens may be in an experiment to see if officeholders and a network of nonpartisan civic organizations promoting dialogue and deliberation can collaborate in jointly framing major policy issues, particularly those that require making difficult trade-offs such as reducing the federal debt. In 2013, people with congressional experience, along with officials from the Treasury and Health and Human Services, met to see if it was possible to develop a framework for public deliberation on deficit reduction.[59] This framework had to address officeholder concerns about what citizens didn't understand and about how people would react to painful trade-offs. The framework also had to reflect the things people held dear and what they felt was at stake. And it had to promote serious choice work on the part of citizens. Obviously, one meeting isn't enough to hammer out a framework and hold deliberative dialogues. That will have to happen over the next 12 months, which will be after this book goes to press. If this experiment—and others like it at the state level—can continue over enough years and on enough issues to overcome the inevitable obstacles, the potential for realignment is considerable.[60]

The Executive Branch

Other realignment experiments to counter mutual distrust have to do directly with administrators and the agencies of government (sometimes called the bureaucracy). Some involve the public deliberations that help counter legislative polarization; they have also helped administrative agencies to cope with gridlock. (Recall Max's story in the first pages of this book.) One of these projects is with state budget officers to see whether online deliberative games can give them a better sense of what citizens value and how citizens would deal with budget trade-offs.[61]

Realignment experiments could also test the assumption that civic work, which produces public goods, can make institutions more productive.[62] Support from the complementary work of citizens should be an incentive to realignment. However, I wouldn't expect professionals' doubts about the citizenry or institutions' defensiveness to disappear. Yet neither institutions nor professionals are immune to change.

I need to say a bit more about citizens producing public goods that benefit not only government agencies but also schools and nongovernmental organizations. I want to reemphasize an important distinction that has to do with the ability of people to exercise greater control over their lives. Democratic realignment has to put more responsibility in the hands of people. Partnership with citizens may or may not do that.

Happily, people often volunteer to help institutions with their work. The institutions decide on the work to be done and citizens are their partners. For example, a group of professional construction engineers might be assisted by citizen volunteers in building a school. This might be called "joint production." Alternatively, professionals might work independently from citizens doing their work, yet the two efforts could complement one another if they have common objectives. I have called this "complementary production." An example would be construction engineers designing a school, and citizens bringing their shovels and rakes to do the landscaping. Complementary production has significant democratic potential because it encourages independent civic initiative. Citizens own and control their work.

Elinor Ostrom, you may remember, demonstrated that the things citizens make can reinforce what the agencies of government do. The importance of complementary production is particularly evident in natural disasters. Studies show that in the first 72 hours after a disaster, survival depends largely on the resilience of neighbors and communities.[63] Government resources can't reach victims when roads are blocked and electricity has been cut off. People have to depend on the work they do with one another.

Neighbors working with neighbors is more important than well-stocked pantries, curative drugs, or economic bailouts. In a word, security is collective. This is why I think the benefits of complementary production could be a powerful incentive for more experiments in institutional realignment.

The Judicial Branch

The decline in public confidence also affects the court system and judges. Americans think we have the best legal system in the world. Still, half of us believe the legal system needs significant reforms.[64] Experiments to respond (and to realign with democratic practices) depend on judicial officials getting a better sense of what and how the citizenry is thinking about the system. The American Bar Association has produced three deliberative issue guides to find out.[65] Outcomes from forums based on these guides have shown that Americans are concerned about the influence of money and worry that judges might become "jaded" and treat cases too routinely, "mass production style."

These perceptions may or may not be valid, but they are the necessary points of reference for any judicial experiments to respond. What those experiments and any realignment will be is an open question at this point. However, the judicial branch has had one of the greatest examples of coproduction: the jury system. That's good news, although it is tempered by a decline in the number of cases going to juries.[66] Still, the reliance on deliberative juries is a precedent for other forms of realignment.

WHERE TO BEGIN?

Conventional wisdom assumes that institutions must change in order to stem the loss of public confidence. Meaningful reforms in schools, government agencies, and nongovernmental organizations would certainly be great. Yet, counterintuitive as it may seem, the key to bridging the divide may be more on the public side of the rift. That is, the best strategy for combating the rampant loss of confidence and legitimacy in institutions may be in strengthening the capacity for civic work. Institutions can't do that work, but they can strengthen it by aligning what they do with it.

The potential is there. Longitudinal studies by Bob Putnam and his colleagues along with one by Vaughn Grisham, who did the study of

Tupelo, Mississippi, show that people are more likely to be satisfied with governments when they aren't so dependent on them.[67] And I would add again that citizens seem to have more confidence in institutions when they are involved with them in complementary production.

This connection between complementary production and institutional legitimacy was illustrated in a study of public schools that looked at people who described themselves as "partners" of the schools, but I think were more. The group was numerically small but substantively quite significant. The citizens involved wanted to take their share of responsibility for young people and did, through a variety of civic projects—some involving joint production and some complementary production. These citizens had a consistently positive view of the public schools. They considered these institutions their agents, not only in educating children *but also in improving their communities*. And the dual goal of improving the community and the schools attracted people who weren't parents; they had a stronger sense that "the well-being of their community is inextricably linked to what goes on in the schools."[68]

Institutions—schools and others—have good reason to do whatever they can to foster the practices that citizens use in doing their work even though people may be more interested in the well-being of their community than any one institution in it. Investing in civic capacity isn't typically on the mission statement of many institutions because, as has been noted, they say it isn't what we do. But maybe it should be.[69]

13
REFLECTIONS

AFTER COMPLETING THIS BOOK, my colleagues and I asked ourselves what we had learned from the experience. We thought our reflecting on that question might spark similar reflections by those of you who read the book. We'd like to hear your thoughts.

What the book has to offer is a different way of looking at what already exists. It doesn't disagree with the dominant understanding of democracy, which is as a system of contested elections to create representative governments. Yet it argues that democracy is more, which is why I've suggested imagining politics as an ecosystem and used a wetlands analogy to describe the often-overlooked realm of citizen politics.

The wetlands analogy calls attention to what is, in one sense, quite common—people talking to one another, citizens working together. That's not difficult to describe. The difficulty has been conveying the extraordinary potential in what appears commonplace and unexceptional—the everyday opportunities for people to shape their future. That potential suggests a different politics, one that isn't so fixed on meeting needs and doing for others as it is on people recognizing their own assets and building on them.

This politics runs into a lot of pushback; that's why the book has so much to say about engaging the critics—if possible not by arguments but by practical experiments. I've tried especially hard to be clear that

I'm *not* saying people don't have needs or that they should pick themselves up by their bootstraps or that the work they do with others will triumph over all else. What the Kettering Foundation has learned *isn't* about how democracy can be made easy. Neither is it about something that people can't do without extensive training or an entirely different set of skills. The book points out the possibilities in doing the ordinary in different ways.

Often the people who have tried doing something routine differently—for instance, making decisions by deliberating—have discovered that they could do far more than they thought they could.[1] They see how they can make a difference by using valuable resources all around them, including the way they talk with other people.

A student who was introduced to deliberative decision making in a college course wrote that what he had learned wasn't just about the practice of deliberating but about himself. He learned his voice had more power than he realized. He could express opinions, weigh options with others, and make better decisions for himself and his community. He felt that his fellow students could create a community that was more than "various individuals squawking over hard pressed issues," a community that was reasonably coherent and reasonably cohesive. And he knew how to make that community stronger: it could begin by joining his voice with others.[2] The small changes that citizens like this student can make by working with other citizens are admittedly incremental and slow to happen. Still, as you have seen, I am impressed that small changes in a dynamic system like the political ecosystem can have far-reaching effects. This possibility was captured in Edward Lorenz's insight that seemingly insignificant events like the flapping of a butterfly's wing in Brazil can have huge, though unpredictable, effects across the globe, perhaps provoking a tornado in Texas.[3] And as someone said in one of the studies cited, just trying to make a difference can be the difference.

The Kettering Foundation has been working on citizen politics for more than three decades. So, while this book is new, it isn't a report on what is new. It's about what is enduring. Citizens, like those cited here, have persisted in trying to find better ways to engage their fellow citizens, to avoid hasty decisions and unproductive conflict, to work together even when they differ, to make use of the resources they have at hand, and to get the Squares to recognize they need the Blobs.

In going through dozens of drafts of this book, I made notations for the next version; often I wrote, "complete this discussion." I really couldn't finish a book on democracy; everything I wrote is open to question and revision. The problems of democracy itself are enduring because they are rooted in human nature. The challenge of combating those problems, however, changes constantly because the circumstances democracy faces vary almost day to day. I continue to look forward to learning what people like the Ruths, Genes, Sandys, Maxes, and Sues will do as they meet new challenges.

I've tried to keep learning because democracy is a political system that depends on learning. There is no acceptable authority on what we as a citizenry *should* do. We have to figure that out ourselves.

NOTES

Introducing the People Who Make Our Democracy Work as It Should

[1] *Newsweek* described these citizens as "The Real Fixers" in its issue of September 19, 2011, 40–42.

[2] The people introduced in the pages that follow are composites of the many citizens the Kettering Foundation has met who live ordinary lives but do extraordinary things.

[3] For research documenting the changing relationship between the public and the public schools, see David Mathews, *Is There a Public for Public Schools?* (Dayton, OH: Kettering Foundation Press, 1996); *Why Public Schools? Whose Public Schools? What Early Communities Have to Tell Us* (Montgomery, AL: NewSouth Books, 2003); and *Reclaiming Public Education by Reclaiming Our Democracy* (Dayton, OH: Kettering Foundation Press, 2006).

[4] City of Dayton, 2012 *Water Quality Report* (Dayton, OH: City of Dayton Department of Water, 2012).

[5] As historian Rush Welter observed, our new nation was able to allow individuals maximum freedom because schools, common to all, would see to it that social order prevailed. Americans opted for a system he described as "anarchy with a schoolmaster." Rush Welter, *Popular Education and Democratic Thought in America* (New York: Columbia University Press, 1962), 4.

PART I. DEMOCRACY RECONSIDERED

1. Systemic Problems of Self-Rule

[1] Dwight D. Eisenhower, "Address Recorded for the Republican Lincoln Day Dinners, January 28, 1954," *Public Papers of the Presidents of the United States: Dwight D. Eisenhower, 1954* (Washington, DC: Office of the Federal Register, National Archives and Records Service, General Services Administration, 1960), 219.

2. Struggling for a Citizen-Centered Democracy

[1] *The Complete Lincoln-Douglas Debates of 1858*, ed. Paul M. Angle (Chicago: University of Chicago Press, 1991), 128.

[2] For more on the meaning of democracy, I suggest Paul Woodruff, *First Democracy* (New York: Oxford University Press, 2005); Giovanni Sartori, *The Theory of Democracy Revisited* (Chatham, NJ: Chatham House Publishers, 1987); Jürgen Habermas, "Three Normative Models of Democracy," *Constellations: An International Journal of Critical and Democratic Theory* (December 1994): 1–10; and Jane Mansbridge, *Beyond Adversary Democracy* (Chicago: University of Chicago Press, 1983).

[3] Robert H. Wiebe, *Self-Rule: A Cultural History of American Democracy* (Chicago: University of Chicago Press, 1995). Also see David Mathews, *Why Public Schools? Whose Public Schools? What Early Communities Have to Tell Us* (Montgomery, AL: NewSouth Books, 2003).

[4] Alexis de Tocqueville, *Democracy in America*, trans. Harvey C. Mansfield and Delba Winthrop (Chicago: University of Chicago Press, 2000), 180–181, 489–490.

[5] Rasmussen Reports, "America's Best Days," http://www.rasmussenreports.com/public_content/politics/mood_of_america/america_s_best_days (accessed September 25, 2013). A Pew Research Center survey found "a perfect storm of conditions associated with distrust of government—a dismal economy, an unhappy public, bitter partisan-based backlash, and epic discontent with Congress and elected officials." See the Pew Research Center's April 18, 2010 report, *Distrust, Discontent, Anger and Partisan Rancor: The People and Their Government*, http://people-press.org/2010/04/18/distrust-discontent-anger-and-partisan-rancor (accessed September 25, 2013).

⁶ Ron Fournier and Sophie Quinton, "In Nothing We Trust," *National Journal*, April 19, 2012, http://www.nationaljournal.com/features/restoration-calls/in-nothing-we-trust-20120419 (accessed August 24, 2012).

⁷ See the chart "Confidence in Institutions Declines" in Fournier and Quinton, "In Nothing We Trust." See also Gallup Poll, *Confidence in Institutions*, June 7–10, 2012, http://www.gallup.com/poll/1597/confidence-institutions.aspx (accessed September 25, 2013).

⁸ Fournier and Quinton, "In Nothing We Trust."

⁹ Fareed Zakaria, *The Post-American World, Release 2.0* (New York: W.W. Norton, 2008), 211.

¹⁰ Jean Johnson, Jonathan Rochkind, and Samantha DuPont, *Don't Count Us Out: How an Overreliance on Accountability Could Undermine the Public's Confidence in Schools, Business, Government, and More* (New York and Dayton, OH: Public Agenda and Kettering Foundation, 2011), 23–24.

¹¹ Daniel Yankelovich, *Coming to Public Judgment: Making Democracy Work in a Complex World* (Syracuse, NY: Syracuse University Press, 1991), 91–98.

¹² As Matt Leighninger reports, "The desire for control is a natural impulse, and it shows up all the time in all kinds of communities"; Matt Leighninger, *The Next Form of Democracy: How Expert Rule Is Giving Way to Shared Governance . . . and Why Politics Will Never Be the Same* (Nashville, TN: Vanderbilt University Press, 2006), 72.

¹³ Jean Johnson, memorandum to Paloma Dallas, Melinda Gilmore, and David Mathews, "Some Additional Material That Might Be Useful for the *Ecology* Book," April 23, 2012.

¹⁴ Johnson, Rochkind, and DuPont, *Don't Count Us Out*, 26.

¹⁵ This sentiment may have earlier origins, but the line "We are the ones we've been waiting for" appears in a 1978 poem by June Jordan titled "Poem for South African Women." In 1995, Bernice Johnson Reagon composed a commissioned work, "Anybody Here? Song Journey in Seven Movements," with text from Jordan's poem. The recessional of the work is a song called "We Are the Ones," which was performed by the group Sweet Honey in the Rock.

¹⁶ National Conference on Citizenship, *Report Shows Majority of Americans Civically Engaged in Their Communities: Boomers and Older Adults Rank High Across Several Key Categories of Civic Engagement* (Washington, DC:

National Conference on Citizenship, September 15, 2011), http://www.ncoc.
net/2011-CLArelease (accessed September 25, 2013).

[17] Sandra L. Hanson and John Kenneth White, "The Making and Persistence of the American Dream," in *The American Dream in the 21st Century*,
ed. Sandra L. Hanson and John Kenneth White (Philadelphia: Temple University Press, 2011), 1–16.

[18] These comments were made by participants in group discussions at the
Kettering Foundation on October 5, 2011 and November 14, 2011.

[19] Richard C. Harwood, *The Work of Hope: How Individuals and Organizations Can Authentically Do Good* (Dayton, OH: Kettering Foundation Press,
2012). Richard Harwood is founder and president of The Harwood Institute
for Public Innovation.

[20] Harwood, *The Work of Hope*, 38.

[21] Ibid., 73–76, 87.

[22] Ibid., 68–69, 73, 76.

[23] Ibid., 78–79.

[24] Christian Meier, *The Greek Discovery of Politics*, trans. David McLintock
(Cambridge, MA: Harvard University Press, 1990), 4–5.

[25] Ray Oldenburg has written about such places in *The Great Good Place:
Cafés, Coffee Shops, Bookstores, Bars, Hair Salons, and Other Hangouts at the
Heart of a Community* (New York: Marlowe, 1999).

[26] Benjamin Barber, *Strong Democracy: Participatory Politics for a New Age*
(Berkeley: University of California Press, 1984); Harry C. Boyte, *The Backyard
Revolution: Understanding the New Citizen Movement* (Philadelphia: Temple
University Press, 1980); Matt Leighninger, *The Next Form of Democracy: How
Expert Rule Is Giving Way to Shared Governance . . . and Why Politics Will
Never Be the Same* (Nashville, TN: Vanderbilt University Press, 2006); Mark
E. Warren, "When, Where and Why Do We Need Deliberation, Voting, and
Other Means of Organizing Democracy? A Problem-Based Approach to
Democratic Systems" (paper prepared for delivery at the American Political
Science Association annual meeting, New Orleans, LA, August 30–September
2, 2012).

[27] Carmen Sirianni and Lewis Friedland, *Civic Innovation in America:
Community Empowerment, Public Policy, and the Movement for Civic Renewal*

(Berkeley: University of California Press, 2001); Peter Levine, *We Are the Ones We Have Been Waiting For: The Promise of Civic Renewal in America* (New York: Oxford University Press, 2013); and Xavier de Souza Briggs, *Democracy as Problem Solving: Civic Capacity in Communities across the Globe* (Cambridge, MA: MIT Press, 2008).

[28] David Mathews, *Politics for People: Finding a Responsible Public Voice*, 2nd ed. (Chicago: University of Illinois Press, 1999), 139.

[29] Briggs, *Democracy as Problem Solving*, 15, 17.

[30] Elinor Ostrom, *Governing the Commons: The Evolution of Institutions for Collective Action* (Cambridge: Cambridge University Press, 1990) and Elinor Ostrom, "Beyond Markets and States: Polycentric Governance of Complex Economic Systems," *American Economic Review* 100, no. 3 (June 2010): 641–672.

[31] Robert Putnam, *Bowling Alone: The Collapse and Revival of American Community* (New York: Simon & Schuster, 2000), 336–349.

[32] Vaughn L. Grisham Jr., *Tupelo: The Evolution of a Community* (Dayton, OH: Kettering Foundation Press, 1999).

[33] The foundation developed its concept of civic work by drawing from what Harry C. Boyte and Nancy N. Kari wrote about public work in *Building America: The Democratic Promise of Public Work* (Philadelphia: Temple University Press, 1996).

[34] See John P. Kretzmann and John L. McKnight, *Building Communities from the Inside Out: A Path Toward Finding and Mobilizing a Community's Assets* (Chicago: ACTA Publications, 1993) as well as John P. Kretzmann and John L. McKnight, *Voluntary Associations in Low-Income Neighborhoods: An Unexplored Community Resource, A Case Study of Chicago's Grand Boulevard Neighborhood* (Evanston, IL: The Asset-Based Community Development Institute, Institute for Policy Research, Northwestern University, 1996).

[35] T. A. Boyd, *Professional Amateur: The Biography of Charles F. Kettering* (New York: E.P. Dutton, 1957), 210.

3. The Political Ecosystem

[1] There is a scholarly literature on complex adaptive systems: See Lance H. Gunderson and C. S. Holling, eds., *Panarchy: Understanding Transformations in Human and Natural Systems* (Washington, DC: Island Press, 2002).

[2] Robert A. Morton, "Historical Changes in the Mississippi-Alabama Barrier-Island Chain and the Roles of Extreme Storms, Sea Level, and Human Activities," *Journal of Coastal Research* (November 2008): 1587–1600. "Historical land-loss trends and engineering records show that progressive increases in land-loss rate correlate with nearly simultaneous deepening of channels dredged across the outer bars of the three tidal inlets maintained for deep-draft shipping," p. 1587.

[3] Ernesto's story is a composite of a number of stories that individuals and civic groups have shared with Kettering over the years.

[4] U.S. Bureau of Labor Statistics, "Volunteering in the United States—2012," news release, February 22, 2013, http://www.bls.gov/news.release/volun.nr0.htm (accessed September 26, 2013).

[5] National CASA – CASA for Children, "Recruiting Volunteers of Color," http://www.casaforchildren.org/site/c.mtJSJ7MPIsE/b.5466357/k.34E3/Recruiting_Volunteers_of_Color.htm (accessed September 26, 2013).

[6] Mary Parker Follett, *The New State: Group Organization the Solution of Popular Government* (New York: Longmans, Green and Company, 1920), 157.

[7] The Institute for Intercultural Studies, which was established by Margaret Mead in 1944, states: "Although the Institute has received many inquiries about this famous admonition by Margaret Mead, we have been unable to locate when and where it was first cited. . . . We believe it probably came into circulation through a newspaper report of something said spontaneously and informally. We know, however, that it was firmly rooted in her professional work and that it reflected a conviction that she expressed often, in different contexts and phrasings." More can be found at http://www.interculturalstudies.org/faq.html (accessed October 18, 2013).

[8] Grassroots politics takes many forms, but in this context I am referring to localized efforts by citizens to influence elections and government action.

[9] Kettering program officer Derek W. M. Barker has analyzed this phenomenon in "The Colonization of Civil Society," in the *Kettering Review* 28, no. 1 (Fall 2010): 8–18, and in "From Associations to Organizations: Tocqueville, NGOs, and the Colonization of Civic Leadership," in *Alexis de Tocqueville and the Art of Democratic Statesmanship*, ed. Brian Danoff and L. Joseph Hebert Jr. (Lanham, MD: Lexington Books, 2011), 205-223.

[10] My views on this were influenced by reading the works of Lawrence E. Susskind.

[11] Edgar S. Cahn, *No More Throw-Away People: The Co-Production Imperative*, 2nd ed. (Washington, DC: Essential Books, 2004). The video can be seen at www.nomorethrowawaypeople.org.

[12] Cahn, *No More Throw-Away People*, 83–84.

[13] George Will cites a case of Blob/Square misalignment in a column about a citizen in Arizona who attempted to get others to join her (forming a Blob) in opposing a bond measure, only to be stopped by a state law requiring that two or more people joined together to influence a vote become a "political committee" (a Square), which had to register, file formally, and establish a bank account. George F. Will, "How States Are Restricting Political Speech," *The Washington Post*, February 1, 2012, http://articles.washingtonpost.com/2012-02-01/opinions/35446037_1_law-firm-political-speech-local-governments (accessed September 26, 2013).

[14] For examples of civic groups developing into government bureaucracies at different points of American history, see Frances Fox Piven and Richard A. Cloward, *Poor People's Movements: Why They Succeed, How They Fail* (New York: Vintage Books, 1979). See also William E. Nelson, *The Roots of American Bureaucracy, 1830-1900* (Cambridge, MA: Harvard University Press, 1982); Charles Postel, *The Populist Vision* (New York: Oxford University Press, 2007); Robert H. Wiebe, *The Search for Order, 1877-1920* (New York: Hill and Wang, 1967), 159–163; and Theda Skocpol, *Protecting Soldiers and Mothers: The Political Origins of Social Policy in the United States* (Cambridge, MA: Belknap Press of Harvard University Press, 1992), esp. 480–524.

[15] See Matt Leighninger, "Is Everything Up to Date in Kansas City? Why 'Citizen Involvement' May Soon Be Obsolete," *National Civic Review* (Summer 2007), esp. 22, 26–27. Also see John Gaventa and Gregory Barrett, *So What Difference Does It Make? Mapping the Outcomes of Citizen Engagement*, IDS Working Paper, 347 (Brighton, UK: Institute of Development Studies, October 2010), 51–52.

[16] Michael Briand and Jane Urschel, *Experiments in Reconnecting Communities and Their Schools: The Boulder Valley Public Schools Public Deliberative Process 1999-2000* (Dayton, OH: Colorado Association of School Boards' Report to the Kettering Foundation, August 2000).

[17] John Gaventa and Gregory Barrett, *So What Difference Does It Make? Mapping the Outcomes of Citizen Engagement*, IDS Working Paper, 347 (Brighton, UK: Institute of Development Studies, October 2010), 52.

[18] Richard C. Harwood and John A. Creighton, *The Organization-First Approach: How Programs Crowd Out Community* (Bethesda, MD: Kettering Foundation and The Harwood Institute for Public Innovation, 2009), 2.

[19] This analysis of the findings was done by Derek W. M. Barker and appeared in "The Colonization of Civil Society," *Kettering Review* 28, no. 1 (Fall 2010): 11.

[20] Ibid., 11.

[21] For this understanding, I've drawn largely from the work of Milton Rokeach and Sandra J. Ball-Rokeach, "Stability and Change in American Value Priorities, 1968-1981," *American Psychologist* 44 (May 1989): 775–784.

[22] See John P. Kretzmann and John L. McKnight, *Building Communities from the Inside Out: A Path toward Finding and Mobilizing a Community's Assets* (Evanston, IL: Center for Urban Affairs and Policy Research, Neighborhood Innovations Network, Northwestern University, 1993).

[23] The best source I have found on covenants is in "Covenant and Polity," by Daniel J. Elazar and John Kincaid, *New Conversations* 4, no. 2 (Fall 1979): 4–8.

[24] Richard C. Harwood, *The Work of Hope: How Individuals and Organizations Can Authentically Do Good* (Dayton, OH: Kettering Foundation Press, 2012).

[25] Theresa Francis, chairperson of UAW Local 1604's Century Brass Steering Committee, in Jeremy Brecher, "'If All the People Are Banded Together': The Naugatuck Valley Project," *Labor Research Review* 1, no. 9, article 10 (1986): 3.

[26] For other examples, see Scott London, *Informal Networks: The Power of Organic Community Groups* (Dayton, OH: A Harwood Institute Report Prepared for the Kettering Foundation, May 2010), available at www.newpossibilitiesassociates.com/uploads/LSF_Informal_Networks_Final.pdf.

PART II. CITIZENS AND COMMUNITIES

4. "Here, Sir, the People Govern." Really?

[1] Jill Lepore, quoting Whitaker in "The Lie Factory: How Politics Became a Business, *The New Yorker* (September 24, 2012), http://www.newyorker.com/reporting/2012/09/24/120924fa_fact_lepore (accessed June 26, 2012).

^{2} Alexander Hamilton, remarks at the New York convention on the adoption of the federal Constitution in 1788. He was referring to the House of Representatives. Jonathan Elliot, *The Debates in the Several State Conventions on the Adoption of the Federal Constitution*, vol. 2 (1836; reprinted, Philadelphia: J.B. Lippincott Company, 1937), 348.

^{3} Walter Lippmann, *The Phantom Public* (1927; reprint, New Brunswick, NJ: Transaction Publishers, 2004).

^{4} Thomas R. Dye, Harmon Zeigler, and Louis Schubert, *The Irony of Democracy: An Uncommon Introduction to American Politics*, 15th ed. (Boston: Wadsworth, Cengage Learning, 2012), 1–2.

^{5} John R. Hibbing and Elizabeth Theiss-Morse, *Stealth Democracy: Americans' Beliefs about How Government Should Work* (New York: Cambridge University Press, 2002).

^{6} This point was made by Albert Dzur in a memorandum to the Kettering Foundation, November 27, 2012. The evidence can be found in Michael A. Neblo et al., "Who Wants to Deliberate—And Why?" *American Political Science Review* 104, no. 3 (August 2010): 566–583 and in Albert W. Dzur, "Four Theses on Participatory Democracy: Toward the Rational Disorganization of Government Institutions," *Constellations* 19, no. 2 (2012): 305–324.

^{7} The Harwood Group, *Squaring Realities: Governing Boards and Community-Building* (Dayton, OH: Kettering Foundation, 2000), 10.

^{8} Richard C. Harwood, *The Work of Hope: How Individuals and Organizations Can Authentically Do Good* (Dayton, OH: Kettering Foundation Press, 2012), 73.

^{9} Bill Bishop with Robert G. Cushing, *The Big Sort: Why the Clustering of Like-Minded America Is Tearing Us Apart* (New York: Houghton Mifflin, 2008), 302.

^{10} John Creighton, memorandum to Kettering Foundation Public-Government workgroup, "Money and Politics Focus Group," September 9, 2011.

^{11} Christopher Dickey, "Citizens, It's Down to You," *Newsweek*, September 21, 2011.

^{12} Richard C. Harwood, *Citizens and Politics: A View from Main Street America* (Dayton, OH: Kettering Foundation, 1991), 3–5, 11–18.

[13] See David Mathews, *Politics for People: Finding a Responsible Public Voice*, 2nd ed. (Chicago: University of Illinois Press, 1999), 11–12.

[14] Ibid., 15–16.

[15] Matthew A. Crenson and Benjamin Ginsberg, *Downsizing Democracy: How America Sidelined Its Citizens and Privatized Its Public* (Baltimore: The Johns Hopkins University Press, 2002), 48.

[16] Theda Skocpol, "The Narrowing of Civic Life," *The American Prospect* (May 17, 2004), http://prospect.org/article/narrowing-civic-life (accessed July 2, 2013).

[17] Ibid.

[18] Theda Skocpol, "Reinventing American Civic Democracy," *Kettering Review* 28 (Fall 2010): 50.

[19] Martha Derthick, "Crossing Thresholds: Federalism in the 1960s," in *Keeping the Compound Republic: Essays on American Federalism* (Washington, DC: Brookings Institution Press, 2001), 152.

[20] Richard C. Harwood, *Hope Unraveled: The People's Retreat and Our Way Back* (Dayton, OH: Kettering Foundation Press, 2005).

[21] Jimmy Carter, "Remarks before the Indian Parliament, January 2, 1978," *Public Papers of the Presidents of the United States, 1978, bk. 1, January 1 to June 30, 1978* (Washington, DC: U.S. Government Printing Office, 1979), 11.

5. Putting the Public Back in the Public's Business

[1] Elliot Richardson, "We Delegated Our Powers" (speech at the Fourth Presidential Library Conference, Gerald R. Ford Library, Ann Arbor, MI, March 18, 1986), 3. Richardson was Secretary of HEW, 1970–1973; Defense Secretary, January–May 1973; Attorney General, May–October 1973; Secretary of Commerce, 1976–1977.

[2] The controversy over what the Constitution meant by sovereignty is discussed in George M. Dennison's *The Dorr War: Republicanism on Trial, 1831-1861* (Lexington: University Press of Kentucky, 1976).

[3] This quotation, popularly attributed to Tocqueville, is a loose translation of a theme of the chapter in *Democracy in America* titled, "On the Use That the Americans Make of Association in Civil Life." See Alexis de Tocqueville, *Democracy in America*, trans. Harvey C. Mansfield and Delba Winthrop

(Chicago: University of Chicago Press, 2000), 489–492. On page 490 of the Mansfield and Winthrop edition, we find the following passage: "Thus the most democratic country on earth is found to be, above all, the one where men in our day have most perfected the art of pursuing the object of their common desires in common and have applied this new science to most objects. . . . Could it be that there in fact exists a necessary relation between associations and equality?"

[4] The Civil Rights Movement is probably the most dramatic example of citizens joining forces. See John Dittmer, *Local People: The Struggle for Civil Rights in Mississippi* (Urbana: University of Illinois Press, 1994). This book documents the work citizens did long before the national movement.

[5] Elena Fagotto and Archon Fung, *Sustaining Public Engagement: Embedded Deliberation in Local Communities* (East Hartford, CT: An Occasional Research Paper from Everyday Democracy and the Kettering Foundation, 2009), 37–41.

[6] The IAF story is in Harry C. Boyte, "The Growth of Citizen Politics: Stages in Local Community Organizing," *Dissent* 37 (Fall 1990): 516.

[7] Although this is often popularly attributed to Martin Luther King Jr., it has also been connected to others active in the Civil Rights Movement.

[8] Edgar Cahn makes this point explicit in his work with time banking. See TimeBanks USA, timebanks.org (accessed July 9, 2013).

[9] Harwood has meticulously traced the way people become involved in public life in two studies: *The Engagement Path: The Realities of How People Engage over Time—and the Possibilities for Re-engaging Americans* (Bethesda, MD: The Harwood Institute, October 2003), and an earlier report by The Harwood Group, *Meaningful Chaos: How People Form Relationships with Public Concerns* (Dayton, OH: Report to the Kettering Foundation, 1993).

[10] A woman from Little Rock did, in fact, help support an anticrime program after finding syringes by the side of her house. The Harwood Group, *Meaningful Chaos: How People Form Relationships with Public Concerns* (Dayton, OH: Report to the Kettering Foundation, 1993), 11–12.

[11] The Harwood Group, *Strategies for Civil Investing: Foundations and Community-Building* (Dayton, OH: Report to the Kettering Foundation, 1997), 8.

[12] Robert H. Wiebe, *Self-Rule: A Cultural History of American Democracy* (Chicago: University of Chicago Press, 1995), 71.

[13] I wrote about the early public schools in *Why Public Schools? Whose Public Schools? What Early Communities Have to Tell Us* (Montgomery, AL: NewSouth Books, 2003).

[14] I've found Paul Woodruff's research on democracy useful. See *First Democracy: The Challenge of an Ancient Idea* (New York: Oxford University Press, 2005).

[15] Elinor Ostrom, "Covenanting, Co-Producing, and the Good Society." *The Newsletter of PEGS (Committee on the Political Economy of the Good Society)* 3, no. 2 (Summer 1993): 7–9.

[16] The classic reference on "wicked" problems is Horst W. J. Rittel and Melvin M. Webber, "Dilemmas in a General Theory of Planning," *Policy Sciences* 4 (1973): 155–169. For more on how this concept is defined in various fields, see Sandra S. Batie, "Wicked Problems and Applied Economics," *American Journal of Agricultural Economics* 90, no. 5 (2008): 1176–1191.

[17] John L. McKnight and John P. Kretzmann call these resources "assets" and describe them in John P. Kretzmann and John L. McKnight, *Building Communities from the Inside Out: A Path Toward Finding and Mobilizing a Community's Assets* (Evanston, IL: Center for Urban Affairs and Policy Research, Neighborhood Innovations Network, Northwestern University, 1993).

[18] A classic study that demonstrates the health benefits of strong social networks was done in Roseto, Pennsylvania. There are several sources. I suggest John G. Bruhn and Stewart Wolf, *The Roseto Story: An Anatomy of Health* (Norman: University of Oklahoma Press, 1979). Also see Marc Pilisuk and Susan Hillier Parks, *The Healing Web: Social Networks and Human Survival* (Hanover, NH: University Press of New England, 1986).

[19] Bobby Milstein, *Hygeia's Constellation: Navigating Health Futures in a Dynamic and Democratic World* (Atlanta, GA: Centers for Disease Control and Prevention, April 15, 2008), 54–57.

[20] Ostrom, "Covenanting, Co-Producing, and the Good Society," 8.

[21] Robert M. Cornett, "Reclaiming Our Children's Learning—A Strategy" (unpublished paper, Kettering Foundation Archives, Dayton, OH, 2006).

[22] See Jack Shelton, *Consequential Learning: A Public Approach to Better Schools* (Montgomery, AL: NewSouth Books, 2005), 51–58, 69–70, 80–91, 100–109.

[23] See a study of the citizens who aren't professional educators but nonetheless teach, in Patricia Moore Harbour's *Community Educators: A Resource for Educating and Developing Our Youth* (Dayton, OH: Kettering Foundation Press, 2012).

[24] Connie Crockett, "Communities as Educators: A Report on the November 2007 Public and Public Education Workshop," *Connections* (2008): 22–24. Also see Merlene Davis, "Beloved Bluegrass-Aspendale Teen Center a Casualty of Budget Cuts," *Lexington Herald-Leader*, May 22, 2011, http://www.kentucky.com/2011/05/22/1748078/merlene-davis-beloved-bluegrass.html (accessed July 10, 2013).

[25] John Doble, memorandum to Damon Higgins and Randa Slim, "Report on CERI Community Leadership Workshop Baton Rouge, LA, 6/23/93," July 19, 1993, 4.

6. Citizens: Involved and Informed?

[1] A Kettering project on political anthropology and etymology has amassed an extensive literature review on ancient humans, which is being collected into a forthcoming paper by Lauren Kolenko, tentatively titled *The Prehistory of Politics.*

[2] Milton Rokeach and Sandra J. Ball-Rokeach coined the terms "terminal and instrumental values" in their research, which they reported in "Stability and Change in American Value Priorities, 1968-1981," *American Psychologist* 44, no. 5 (May 1989): 775–784.

[3] Wendell Berry, *The Unsettling of America: Culture and Agriculture* (San Francisco: Sierra Club Books, 1986), viii.

[4] This insight came from the results of forums using an issue guide, *Too Many Children Left Behind: How Can We Close the Achievement Gap?* This guide was prepared and published in 2007 by the Kettering Foundation for use in a two-year study. The results were published in a report, *Helping Students Succeed: Communities Confront the Achievement Gap* (Dayton, OH: Kettering Foundation, 2010).

[5] A similar account was shared by a journalist from Alabama during a meeting at the Kettering Foundation on November 16, 2010.

[6] See Ben Seymour and Ray Dolan, "Emotion, Decision Making, and the Amygdala," *Neuron* 58 (June 12, 2008): 662–671; also see Gilles Fauconnier

and Mark Turner, *The Way We Think: Conceptual Blending and the Mind's Hidden Complexities* (New York: Basic Books, 2002).

[7] These conditions for optimal decision making are recognized in the training of flight crews and surgical teams. Crew resource management aims to ensure that everyone present, not just the pilot or surgeon, is involved in recognizing that a problem exists, defining the problem, identifying probable solutions, and taking appropriate action. Jerry Mulenburg, "Crew Resource Management Improves Decision Making," *Ask Magazine: The NASA Source for Project Management and Engineering Excellence* 42 (Spring 2011): 11–13.

[8] Woodrow Wilson, *The New Freedom: A Call for the Emancipation of the Generous Energies of a People* (New York: Doubleday, Page and Company, 1913), 91, 105.

7. Public Deliberation and Public Judgment

[1] In the "Funeral Oration of Pericles," Pericles describes public deliberation as *prodidacthenai . . . logo*, or the talk Athenians use to teach themselves before they act. See Thucydides, *History of the Peloponnesian War* 2.40.2.

[2] Isocrates, "Antidosis," in *Isocrates*, trans. George Norlin, vol. 2 (1929; reprint, New York: G.P. Putnam's Sons, 2000), 179–365 and Aristotle, *The Ethics of Aristotle: The Nicomachean Ethics*, trans. J. A. K. Thomson (London: Penguin Books, reprinted 1956), 84–87, 176–184.

[3] Kettering research is used to prepare deliberative guides for NIF forums but the foundation doesn't hold these forums. That is done by civic, religious, and educational groups. The objective of the guides and the forums is to model sound decision making and "jump start" public deliberation in all the places where decisions are made.

[4] See the National Issues Forums website for a list of reports on these forums at http://www.nifi.org/reports/issues.aspx.

[5] Bonnie Braun et al., *Engaging Unheard Voices: Under What Conditions Can, and Will, Limited Resource Citizens Engage in the Deliberative Public Policy Process?* (College Park, MD: Report to the Kettering Foundation, March 2006), 5.

[6] For an account of the various purposes and concepts of "deliberation," see *Democratizing Deliberation: A Political Theory Anthology*, ed. Derek W. M. Barker, Noëlle McAfee, and David W. McIvor (Dayton, OH: Kettering Foundation Press, 2012).

[7] David Brown, memorandum to David Mathews, "Decision Making and Collective Action," September 1, 2004.

[8] Jane Mansbridge, "Everyday Talk in the Deliberative System," in *Deliberative Politics: Essays on Democracy and Disagreement*, ed. Stephen Macedo (Oxford: Oxford University Press, 1999), 211–239.

[9] Amy Gutmann and Dennis Thompson, *Why Deliberative Democracy?* (Princeton, NJ: Princeton University Press, 2004), 10.

[10] Mansbridge, "Everyday Talk in the Deliberative System," 211–239.

[11] Isocrates, "Antidosis."

[12] Harold Perkin found the Achilles' heel of professionalism in an attitude he describes as "condescension towards the laity." Harold Perkin, *The Rise of Professional Society: England since 1880* (New York: Routledge, 1990), 390.

[13] Martha Derthick, *The Influence of Federal Grants: Public Assistance in Massachusetts* (Cambridge, MA: Harvard University Press, 1970), 79, 158–159.

[14] See an account of the history of national health insurance proposals in John W. Kingdon, *Agendas, Alternatives, and Public Policies*, 2nd ed. (New York: Addison-Wesley Educational Publishers, 2003), 6–9.

[15] Benjamin I. Page and Robert Y. Shapiro, *The Rational Public: Fifty Years of Trends in Americans' Policy Preferences* (Chicago: University of Chicago Press, 1992).

[16] Philip Geyelin, "Dean Rusk's Pursuit of Peace," *Washington Post*, February 8, 1984.

[17] Daniel Yankelovich and Will Friedman, eds., *Toward Wiser Public Judgment* (Nashville, TN: Vanderbilt University Press, 2010), 34.

8. Framing Issues to Encourage Deliberation

[1] For more on this subject, see *Naming and Framing Difficult Issues to Make Sound Decisions: A Kettering Foundation Report* (Dayton, OH: Kettering Foundation, 2011).

[2] See Antonio Damasio, *Descartes' Error: Emotion, Reason, and the Human Brain* (New York: Penguin Books, 2005); also see Benedetto De Martino et al., "Frames, Biases, and Rational Decision-Making in the Human Brain," *Science* 313, no. 5787 (August 4, 2006): 684–687.

[3] Doble Research Associates, *Protecting Our Rights: What Goes on the Internet? NIF Report on the Issues* (Englewood Cliffs, NJ: John Doble Research Associates, 1999), 3.

[4] For more information on citizen-led framing, see *Naming and Framing Difficult Issues.*

9. Opportunities in Communities

[1] Xavier de Souza Briggs, *Democracy as Problem Solving: Civic Capacity in Communities across the Globe* (Cambridge, MA: MIT Press, 2008).

[2] John Dewey, *The Public and Its Problems: An Essay in Political Inquiry*, ed. Melvin L. Rogers (University Park: Pennsylvania State University Press, 2012), 157.

[3] Note that the sharp distinction between what is local and what isn't is challenged in recent scholarly works. Sampson writes about neighborhood effects that are "simultaneously local and extralocal in nature." Robert J. Sampson, *Great American City: Chicago and the Enduring Neighborhood Effect* (Chicago: University of Chicago Press, 2012), 357.

[4] Ibid.

[5] The Suggsville story is drawn from more than 50 communities. These include Tupelo, Mississippi, as described by Vaughn L. Grisham Jr. in *Tupelo: The Evolution of a Community* (Dayton, OH: Kettering Foundation Press, 1999) and Uniontown, Alabama, as described by Joe A. Sumners, with Christa Slaton and Jeremy Arthur, in *Building Community: The Uniontown Story* (Dayton, OH: Report to the Kettering Foundation, 2005). Also see the Kettering publication *For Communities to Work* (Dayton, OH: Kettering Foundation, 2002).

[6] The practices presented here are based on insights about how democracy *should* work. The practices are real; that is, all have occurred at various times in many different places. The way they are described by Kettering, however, reflects the foundation's conceptualization of experience.

[7] The concept of stages in deliberation comes from Daniel Yankelovich, *Coming to Public Judgment: Making Democracy Work in a Complex World* (Syracuse, NY: Syracuse University Press, 1991).

[8] Daniel Yankelovich, "The New Pragmatism: Coping with America's Overwhelming Problems" (lecture, Drucker School of Management at Claremont Graduate University, Claremont, California, November 8, 2008).

[9] These questions came out of the Solomon Project, which worked with low-income communities in Minneapolis to "recognize their own educational capacities." See *The Solomon Project Annual Report* (Minneapolis: Project Public Life, Hubert Humphrey Institute of Public Affairs, 1992). The Solomon results are currently being retested in a project for Kettering led by Patricia Moore Harbour.

[10] Woodrow Wilson, "Address to the Woodrow Wilson Working Men's Dinner, New York City, September 4," in John Wells Davidson, ed., *A Crossroads of Freedom: The 1912 Campaign Speeches of Woodrow Wilson* (New Haven, CT: Yale University Press, 1956), 108.

[11] Monica Schoch-Spana et al., "Community Engagement: Leadership Tool for Catastrophic Health Events," *Biosecurity and Bioterrorism: Biodefense Strategy, Practice and Science* 5, no. 1 (2007): 8–25.

[12] See E. E. Evans-Pritchard, *The Nuer: A Description of the Modes of Livelihood and Political Institutions of a Nilotic People* (New York: Oxford University Press, 1969).

[13] Richard C. Harwood, *The Work of Hope: How Individuals and Organizations Can Authentically Do Good* (Dayton, OH: Kettering Foundation Press, 2012).

[14] For more on different kinds of trust, see Robert D. Putnam, *Bowling Alone: The Collapse and Revival of American Community* (New York: Simon and Schuster, 2000), 134–147 and Robert D. Putnam and Lewis M. Feldstein, *Better Together: Restoring the American Community* (New York: Simon and Schuster, 2003). Putnam distinguishes between "political trust" and "social trust." Also see Janice L. Bockmeyer, "A Culture of Distrust: The Impact of Local Political Culture on Participation in the Detroit EZ," *Urban Studies* 37, no. 13 (December 2000): 2417–2440 and Wendy M. Rahn and Thomas J. Rudolph, "A Tale of Political Trust in American Cities," *Public Opinion Quarterly* 69, no. 4 (Winter 2005): 530–560.

[15] Clarence N. Stone, "Linking Civic Capacity and Human Capital Formation," in *Strategies for School Equity: Creating Productive Schools in a Just Society*, ed. Marilyn J. Gittell (New Haven, CT: Yale University Press, 1998), 163–176.

[16] Kettering researchers studied the work of scholars such as Donald Schön, Chris Argyris, Peter Senge, and Stewart Ranson on learning systems or practices. Although much of their work has explored how organizations learn and how they might learn more productively, it has offered important insights

for community or public learning, particularly the concept of double-loop learning, in which organizations not only review how well they achieved their goals but also whether they had selected the appropriate goals.

[17] Hannah Arendt, *Between Past and Future: Eight Exercises in Political Thought* (New York: Penguin Books, 1977), 220–221.

[18] Kipling calls triumph and disaster two imposters in his poem "If—." Rudyard Kipling, "If—," Poems and Poets, Poetry Foundation, http://www. poetryfoundation.org/poem/175772 (accessed September 24, 2013).

[19] John P. Kretzmann and John L. McKnight, *Building Communities from the Inside Out: A Path Toward Finding and Mobilizing a Community's Assets* (Evanston, IL: Center for Urban Affairs and Policy Research, Neighborhood Innovations Network, Northwestern University, 1993).

[20] J. Herman Blake is a professor, scholar, and administrator and has been an associate of the Kettering Foundation. Throughout his career, Dr. Blake has focused particularly on academic achievement of students from minority and/or low-wealth communities.

10. Democratic Practices

[1] I find Peter Levine's comparison of micro or small-scale efforts with large-scale or macro efforts very useful. See Peter Levine, "Two Levels of Politics," A Blog for Civic Renewal, March 22, 2005, http://www.peterlevine.ws/mt/ archives/2005/03/two-levels-of-p.html (accessed July 22, 2013).

[2] John L. McKnight, *The Four-Legged Stool* (Dayton, OH: A Study for the Kettering Foundation, 2013).

[3] Carne Ross, *The Leaderless Revolution: How Ordinary People Will Take Power and Change Politics in the Twenty-first Century* (New York: Blue Rider Press, 2011), xvii.

[4] Sean Safford, *Why the Garden Club Couldn't Save Youngstown: The Transformation of the Rust Belt* (Cambridge, MA: Harvard University Press, 2009).

[5] Sean Safford, *Why the Garden Club Couldn't Save Youngstown: Civic Infrastructure and Mobilization in Economic Crises*, IPC Working Paper Series (Cambridge, MA: MIT, March 2004), 2. Safford later published this research in a book with a similar title.

[6] The foundation continues to see the importance of the widely dispersed, entrepreneurial leadership that was identified by The Harwood Group in

Forming Public Capital: Observations from Two Communities (Dayton, OH: Report to the Kettering Foundation, August 1995), 5. See also Suzanne W. Morse's chapter, "Growing Leaders," in *Smart Communities: How Citizens and Local Leaders Can Use Strategic Thinking to Build a Brighter Future* (San Francisco: Jossey-Bass, 2004), 181–206.

[7] Robert J. Sampson, *Great American City: Chicago and the Enduring Neighborhood Effect* (Chicago: University of Chicago Press, 2012), 222.

[8] Henrik Ibsen, *An Enemy of the People* (New York: Dover Publications, 1999), 9.

PART III. INSTITUTIONS, PROFESSIONALS, AND THE PUBLIC

11. Bridging the Great Divide

[1] Harris Poll, May 21, 2012. Participants in the poll were asked, "As far as people in charge of running are concerned, would you say you have a great deal of confidence, only some confidence, or hardly any confidence at all in them?" The only institutional leaders with 50 percent or more confidence were in the military (57 percent) and small business (50 percent).

[2] Harris Poll, May 21, 2012.

[3] I found this to be especially true of people's relationship with schools and wrote about it in *Reclaiming Public Education by Reclaiming Our Democracy* (Dayton, OH: Kettering Foundation Press, 2006).

[4] John W. Gardner, *In Common Cause: Citizen Action and How It Works* (New York: W.W. Norton, 1972), 111.

[5] Max Weber, *Economy and Society*, ed. Guenther Roth and Claus Wittich (Berkeley: University of California Press, 1978), 67.

[6] James C. Scott, *Seeing Like a State: How Certain Schemes to Improve the Human Condition Have Failed* (New Haven, CT: Yale University Press, 1998).

[7] "American Democracy: Building the Perfect Citizen," *The Economist* (August 22, 1998): 21–22.

[8] Woodrow Wilson, "The Study of Administration," *Political Science Quarterly* 2 (June 1887) as reproduced in Jay M. Shafritz and Albert C. Hyde, eds., *Classics of Public Administration*, 2nd ed. (Chicago: The Dorsey Press, 1987), 22. Wilson went on to say that, as a practical matter, it wasn't possible

to do what he advocated, but still argued that government administration should be an instrument serving ends established not directly by the people, but by the laws of representative government. See Brian J. Cook, *Democracy and Administration: Woodrow Wilson's Ideas and the Challenges of Public Management* (Baltimore: The Johns Hopkins University Press, 2007), 90.

[9] Martha Derthick, *The Influence of Federal Grants: Public Assistance in Massachusetts* (Cambridge, MA: Harvard University Press, 1970), 71–97, 129, 145–147, 155–157. Derthick talks about "values" not priorities, but I don't use her terminology because I have already defined "values" in a different way.

[10] For example, see the "Code of Ethics" published by the Society of Professional Journalists, www.spj.org/ethicscode.asp (accessed August 20, 2013). "Members of the Society of Professional Journalists believe that public enlightenment is the forerunner of justice and the foundation of democracy. The duty of the journalist is to further those ends by seeking truth and providing a fair and comprehensive account of events and issues."

[11] For an analysis of the accountability movement, see Melvin J. Dubnick and H. George Frederickson, *Accountable Governance: Problems and Promises* (New York: M.E. Sharpe, 2011).

[12] *Will It Be on the Test? A Closer Look at How Leaders and Parents Think about Accountability in the Public Schools* (New York and Dayton: Public Agenda and Kettering Foundation, 2013).

[13] Christopher Pollitt, "Performance Blight and the Tyranny of Light? Accountability in Advanced Performance Measurement Regimes" (paper for the Kettering seminar, Dayton, Ohio, May 22–23, 2008), 19.

[14] *Will It Be on the Test?*

[15] *Will It Be on the Test?* and Sheila A. Arens, *Examining the Meaning of Accountability: Reframing the Construct, a Report on the Perceptions of Accountability* (Aurora, CO: Mid-continent Research for Education and Learning, July 2005).

[16] Arens, *Examining the Meaning of Accountability*.

[17] David Ellerman "Good Intentions: The Dilemma of Outside-In Help for Inside-Out Change," *The Nonprofit Quarterly* (Fall 2006): 46.

[18] Richard C. Harwood and John A. Creighton, *The Organization-First Approach: How Programs Crowd Out Community* (Bethesda, MD: Kettering Foundation and The Harwood Institute for Public Innovation, 2009).

[19] H. George Frederickson writes about the pitfalls of this phenomenon with organizations in *Easy Innovation and the Iron Cage: Best Practice, Benchmarking, Ranking, and the Management of Organizational Creativity* (Dayton, OH: Kettering Foundation, June 2003).

[20] Brian J. Cook, *Bureaucracy and Self-Government: Reconsidering the Role of Public Administration in American Politics* (Baltimore, MD: Johns Hopkins University Press, 1996), 134–135.

[21] Albert Dzur, memorandum to Kettering Foundation, November 27, 2012.

[22] Andrew Gilligan, "A Government Ruse That's Nothing Short of an Insultation," *Telegraph*, August 20, 2010, http://www.telegraph.co.uk/news/politics/7955561/A-Government-ruse-thats-nothing-short-of-an-insultation.html (accessed August 21, 2013).

[23] Pasi Sahlberg, director of the Finnish Ministry of Education's Center for International Mobility, stated, "There's no word for accountability in Finnish . . . Accountability is something that is left when responsibility has been subtracted." Anu Partanen, "What Americans Keep Ignoring about Finland's School Success," *The Atlantic* (December 29, 2011), http://www.theatlantic.com/national/archive/2011/12/what-americans-keep-ignoring-about-finlands-school-success/250564/ (accessed August 21, 2013).

[24] John Gaventa and Gregory Barrett, *So What Difference Does It Make? Mapping the Outcomes of Citizen Engagement*, IDS Working Paper, 347 (Brighton, UK: Institute of Development Studies, October 2010), 27–32, 36, 41.

[25] Frye Gaillard, Sheila Hagler, and Peggy Denniston, *In the Path of the Storms: Bayou La Batre, Coden, and the Alabama Coast* (Auburn, AL: Pebble Hill Books, Auburn University; Tuscaloosa, AL: The University of Alabama Press, 2008).

12. Experiments in Realignment and Possibilities for Experiments

[1] The foundation is happy to share the stories that follow. Yet, as I've said, Kettering isn't an authority on how institutions do their work or how various professionals see their roles. They are the only ones who can answer the how-to questions. The foundation can only suggest what seem to be promising institutional and professional initiatives that might bring about a better alignment.

[2] Kettering's work with journalists benefited enormously from the leadership provided by Kay Fanning, who was a Kettering board member from 1989 to 2000. Kay led the *Anchorage Daily News*, which, under her stewardship, won a Pulitzer Prize for Public Service. She also served as editor of the *Christian Science Monitor* from 1983 to 1988, and in 1987, was the first woman to serve as president of the American Society of Newspaper Editors.

[3] Cole C. Campbell, "Journalism and Public Knowledge," *Kettering Review* (Winter 2007): 39–49. More of Cole's writing is collected in Tony Wharton, ed., *Journalism as a Democratic Art: Selected Essays by Cole C. Campbell* (Dayton, OH: Kettering Foundation Press, 2012).

[4] These questions are similar to one posed by Jay Rosen and later reported in *What Are Journalists For?* (New Haven, CT: Yale University Press, 1999). Rosen was asking, in effect, if the job of the press is to inform the public and there is no public, then what is the job of the press?

[5] "The only way . . . for the community to be a better place to live is for the people of the community to understand and accept their personal responsibility for what happens." Davis "Buzz" Merritt Jr., December 1992. From the unpublished transcript of the Public Journalism Seminar, conducted by the Kettering Foundation and New Directions for News, p. 13.

[6] Davis "Buzz" Merritt's June 12, 1994, speech at The American Press Institute, included in *Speaking of Public Journalism: Talks from the Project on Public Life and the Press—Seminars at the American Press Institute*, 1993-1997 (Dayton, OH: Kettering Foundation, 1997), 21.

[7] Daniel Yankelovich, *Coming to Public Judgment: Making Democracy Work in a Complex World* (Syracuse, NY: Syracuse University Press, 1991), 95–96.

[8] In the late 1980s and early 1990s, journalists like Cole Campbell and Buzz Merritt, along with Jack Swift, executive editor of the *Ledger-Enquirer* in Columbus, Georgia, and others, joined forces with publishers like Jim Batten of Knight Ridder and scholars like Jay Rosen to encourage journalists to do experiments treating readers as citizens. They called what they were doing "public journalism."

[9] Memorandum to Phil Currie, Mark Silverman, and Jay Rosen from Randy Hammer (*Springfield News-Leader*) regarding, "A little backlash to public journalism," December 6, 1995. The memo is on file at the Kettering Foundation archive. Also see Pat Ford, *Don't Stop There! Five Adventures in*

Civic Journalism, ed. Jan Schaffer (Washington, DC: The Pew Center for Civic Journalism, 1998).

[10] The Public Issues Forums of Centre County have collaborated with their local paper, the *Centre Daily Times*, to encourage community deliberation on many local problems.

[11] "Tight Times, Tough Choices," a participatory budgeting project, was organized by the Penn Project for Civic Engagement and the radio/television station WHYY. The Penn Project for Civic Engagement is a project of the University of Pennsylvania that collaborates with media, business, and community agencies to focus on issues in the local community.

[12] Jay Rosen, "The People Formerly Known as the Audience," *Huffington Post*, June 30, 2006, http://www.huffingtonpost.com/jay-rosen/the-people-formerly-known_1_b_24113.html (accessed September 26, 2012). Also see Dan Gillmor, "The Former Audience Joins the Party," *We the Media: Grassroots Journalism by the People, for the People* (Sebastopol, CA: O'Reilly Media, 2004), 136–157, http://www.authorama.com/we-the-media-8.html (accessed September 26, 2012).

[13] I don't want to overstate this distinction. Derek Barker, a program officer at Kettering, points out that the academy sees itself as educating in values and other forms of subjective thought, embodied primarily in the humanities disciplines, for example. But humanistic inquiry in the academy typically applies only in broad, universally acceptable terms. Derek writes, "Since Kant's critique of practical reason, it has been very difficult for experts to talk about having 'knowledge' in moral matters. Kant's critique argued that the only certain principle of morality is the categorical imperative (essentially 'do unto others as others would do unto you'); how this principle is applied is subjective and up to any free individual to determine. Higher education affirms this by dividing inquiry into the scientific disciplines and the humanities. This means that value inquiry must be strictly separated from science, and the humanities must be limited to fundamental principles so as not to be 'politicized.'" Derek Barker, memorandum to Laura Carlson, September 16, 2013.

[14] Isocrates, "Antidosis," in *Isocrates*, trans. George Norlin, vol. 2 (1929; reprint, New York: G.P. Putnam's Sons, 2000), 179–365; Thucydides, *History of the Peloponnesian War* 2.40.2; and Aristotle, *The Ethics of Aristotle: The Nicomachean Ethics*, trans. J. A. K. Thomson (London: Penguin Books, 1953).

[15] Alejandro Sanz de Santamaría, "Education for Political Life," *Kettering Review* (Winter 1993): 9–18.

[16] This kind of alignment isn't confined to any one field. For instance, Harry Boyte, founder and codirector of the Center for Democracy and Citizenship at Augsburg College, has also been a leader in this movement exploring the democratic mission of higher education.

[17] Theodore R. Alter, "Achieving the Promise of Public Scholarship," in *Engaging Campus and Community: The Practice of Public Scholarship in the State and Land-Grant University System*, ed. Scott J. Peters et al. (Dayton, OH: Kettering Foundation Press, 2005), 461–487; Scott J. Peters, with Theodore R. Alter and Neil Schwartzbach, *Democracy and Higher Education: Traditions and Stories of Civic Engagement* (East Lansing, MI: Michigan State University Press, 2010); Frank A. Fear et al., *Coming to Critical Engagement: An Autoethnographic Exploration* (Lanham, MD: University Press of America, 2006). Also see the publications of Ron Hustedde at the University of Kentucky.

[18] Encouraged by then-president Bill Muse and vice president David Wilson, professors Robert Montjoy and Christa Slaton, along with graduate assistants, realigned their work with civic work in a small rural community in Alabama.

[19] Not all of these centers are on college and university campuses but, since this is a discussion of experiments in academe, I have concentrated on those that are. For more information on all types of centers, see Scott London, *Doing Democracy: How a Network of Grassroots Organizations Is Strengthening Community, Building Capacity, and Shaping a New Kind of Civic Education* (Dayton, OH: Kettering Foundation, 2010).

[20] There are several other community-based centers without direct higher education connections, e.g., the Chiesman Center for Democracy in South Dakota, the Hampton Roads Center for Civic Engagement in Virginia, and Iowa Partners in Learning.

[21] These centers can all be found online: www.hofstra.edu/Academics/Colleges/HCLAS/CCE/, www.wipps.org, and www.mathewscenter.org.

[22] *Foundations for Opportunities: 2011 Teacher Institute Programs and Planning*, Michael D'Innocenzo and Bernie Stein for Hofstra University Center for Civic Engagement (September 2011); *Teacher Institute #2 Report 2011*, Jon Lodge for Public Issues Forum of Centre County (PIFCC) and State College Area School District Community Education (SCASD) (September 2011); *The Impact of Deliberative Processes in the Secondary School Setting*, John E. Greenwood, Program Manager, for The Wisconsin Institute for Public

Policy and Service (August 2011); and *Birmingham National Issues Forums in the Classroom Second Six Months Report 2011*, Peggy Sparks, Report to the Kettering Foundation (January 2012).

[23] Katy J. Harriger and Jill J. McMillan, "Public Scholarship and Faculty Role Conflict," *Higher Education Exchange* (2005): 17–23. Also see Katy J. Harriger and Jill J. McMillan, *Speaking of Politics: Preparing College Students for Democratic Citizenship through Deliberative Dialogue* (Dayton, OH: Kettering Foundation Press, 2007).

[24] Other studies show that college students welcome opportunities to engage in deliberations. See Abby Kiesa et al., *Millennials Talk Politics: A Study of College Student Political Engagement* (College Park, MD: CIRCLE, The Center for Information & Research on Civic Learning & Engagement, 2007).

[25] Mark Wilson and Nan Fairley, "Living Democracy: A Project for Students and Citizens," *Higher Education Exchange* (2012): 35–47.

[26] One example of such a critique is included in Bryan Goodwin and Sheila A. Arens, *No Community Left Behind? An Analysis of the Potential Impact of the No Child Left Behind Act of 2001 on School-Community Relationships* (Dayton, OH: McREL Report to the Kettering Foundation, May 2003) 7–8.

[27] National School Public Relations Association, *NSPRA/Kettering Public Engagement Project: Final Report for July 2002-December 2003* (Dayton, OH: Report to the Kettering Foundation, 2003).

[28] Anne T. Henderson and Karen L. Mapp, *A New Wave of Evidence: The Impact of School, Family, and Community Connections on Student Achievement* (Austin, TX: Southwest Educational Development Laboratory, 2002), 54.

[29] Sheila Beachum Bilby, "Community School Reform: Parents Making a Difference in Education," *Mott Mosaic* 1 (December 2002): 3.

[30] Annenberg Institute on Public Engagement for Public Education, *Reasons for Hope, Voices for Change* (Providence, RI: Annenberg Institute for School Reform, 1998). For a discussion of civic capacity building to strengthen the practices citizens use to govern themselves, see Jolley Bruce Christman and Amy Rhodes, *Civic Engagement and Urban School Improvement: Hard-to-Learn Lessons from Philadelphia* (Philadelphia: PA: Consortium for Policy Research in Education, 2002).

[31] Stone cited John Goodlad and others as leading the way among educators and drew examples from the Industrial Areas Foundation (IAF) and

the organizing work of Ernesto Cortes. Clarence N. Stone, "The Dilemmas of Social Reform Revisited: Putting Civic Engagement in the Picture" (paper presented at the annual meeting of the American Political Science Association, Atlanta, GA, September 2–5, 1999). For more on IAF, see Mark R. Warren, *Dry Bones Rattling: Community Building to Revitalize American Democracy* (Princeton, NJ: Princeton University Press, 2001). Also see Robert D. Putnam and Lewis M. Feldstein, *Better Together: Restoring the American Community* (New York: Simon & Shuster, 2003) for IAF and similar examples.

[32] Patricia Moore Harbour, *Community Educators: A Resource for Education and Developing Our Youth* (Dayton, OH: Kettering Foundation Press, 2012).

[33] Marion Brady, "Thinking Big: A Conceptual Framework for the Study of Everything," *Phi Delta Kappan* (December 2004): 276–281.

[34] Peter Levine, "Learning and Democracy: Civic Education," *Kettering Review* (Fall 2006): 32–42.

[35] Campaign for the Civic Mission of Schools, http://www.civicmissionof-schools.org/ (accessed October 5, 2012).

[36] Libby Sander, "Auburn Students Become Small-Town Citizens for the Summer," *The Chronicle of Higher Education* (June 9, 2012), http://chronicle.com/article/article-content/132769 (accessed June 21, 2013).

[37] Stacie Molnar-Main, with Libby Kingseed, "Public Learning in Public Schools: How Networks of Teachers and Public Partners Can Support Civic Learning," *Connections* (2013): 28–30. *The Teacher's Guide to National Issues Forums (NIF) in the Classroom*, along with other materials about students deliberating, can be found on the NIFI website: http://www.nifi.org/issue_books/guides.aspx?catID=3238.

[38] Clarence N. Stone, "Linking Civic Capacity and Human Capital Formation," in *Strategies for School Equity: Creating Productive Schools in a Just Society*, ed. Marilyn J. Gittell (New Haven, CT: Yale University Press, 1998), 163.

[39] For more on out-of-school influences, see James P. Comer, *Waiting for a Miracle: Why Schools Can't Solve Our Problems—And How We Can* (New York: Dutton, 1997).

[40] Randall Nielsen, "Public Schools and the Practices of Engaged Communities," *Connections* (April 2004): 20. The Pueblo case study is also included in

Colorado Association of School Boards, *Public Engagement in Five Colorado School Communities* (Dayton, OH: Report to the Kettering Foundation, 2003), 7–8.

[41] Doble Research Associates, *Expectations and Realities: An Analysis of Existing Research* (Dayton, OH: Report to the Kettering Foundation, January 2004), 27.

[42] Robert D. Putnam, "Community-Based Social Capital and Educational Performance," in *Making Good Citizens: Education and Civil Society*, ed. Diane Ravitch and Joseph P. Viteritti (New Haven, CT: Yale University Press, 2001), 72, 81–82.

[43] Robert M. Cornett, "Reclaiming Our Children's Learning—A Strategy," (unpublished paper, Kettering Foundation Archives, Dayton, OH, 2006). Other community resources used to educate included a bluegrass festival and a project to reintroduce chestnut trees into the Appalachian Mountains. The efforts involved a great many adults who were neither teachers nor parents.

[44] Doble Research Associates, *Take Charge Workshop Series: Descriptions and Findings from the Field* (Dayton, OH: Report to the Kettering Foundation, 1993), 3. The Doble report found that asking people to "map the places of learning in their community has proven to be a very powerful and transformative exercise."

[45] See Heather Harding, "Supplementary Education: Educating and Developing the Whole Child, An Interview with Edmund W. Gordon," *Understanding Educational Equity and Excellence at Scale* (Providence, RI: A Project of the Annenberg Institute for School Reform at Brown University, January 2007), 8–9.

[46] Lawrence A. Cremin, *American Education: The Colonial Experience, 1607-1783* (New York: Harper and Row, 1970); Lawrence A. Cremin, *American Education: The National Experience, 1783-1876* (New York: Harper and Row, 1980); and Lawrence A. Cremin, *American Education: The Metropolitan Experience, 1876-1980* (New York: Harper and Row, 1988).

[47] Edmund W. Gordon and Michael A. Rebell, "Toward a Comprehensive System of Education for All Children," *Teachers College Record* 109, no. 7 (2007): 1836–1843.

[48] Alonzo A. Crim, "A Community of Believers Creates a Community of Achievers," *Educational Record* 68/69 (fall 1987/winter 1988): 45.

[49] Harbour, *Community Educators*, 130–131. For more on cultural strategies, see Nan Kari and Nan Skelton, *Voices of Hope: The Story of the Jane Addams School for Democracy* (Dayton, OH: Kettering Foundation Press, 2007), 27–33, 42–51.

[50] Harbour, *Community Educators*, 63, 95–97, 107–109, 129–130.

[51] Bruce R. Sievers, *Civil Society, Philanthropy, and the Fate of the Commons* (Medford, MA: Tufts University Press, 2010). See also Bruce Sievers, "Can Philanthropy Solve the Problems of Civil Society?" *Kettering Review* (December 1977): 62–70.

[52] A group of local foundations have formed an organization called Grassroots Grantmakers. I heard the expression "start small and stay small" when meeting with this group and its director, Janis Foster Richardson.

[53] See Peter H. Pennekamp and Anne Focke, *Philanthropy and the Regeneration of Community Democracy* (Dayton, OH: Kettering Foundation, 2013).

[54] Allan Comp and Stacy Bouchard, *Exploring the Relationships between Citizen-Led Watershed Groups and Government Institutions* (Dayton, OH: Report to the Kettering Foundation, December 3, 2008).

[55] David Mathews, "Creating a Movement toward 'Civil Philanthropy,'" *The Chronicle of Philanthropy* 7 (April 20, 1995): 42–43. See also Scott London, *Investing in Public Life: A Report from the 2003-2004 Dialogues on Civil Investing* (Dayton, OH: Kettering Foundation and Pew Partnership for Civic Change, 2005).

[56] Aristotle, *The Complete Works of Aristotle*, ed. Jonathan Barnes, trans. Benjamin Jowett, vol. 2 (Princeton, NJ: Princeton University Press, 1984), 2050.

[57] LeRoy Collins et al., *The Mazes of Modern Government: The States, the Legislature, the Bureaucracy, the Courts* (Santa Barbara, CA: Center for the Study of Democratic Institutions of the Fund for the Republic, 1964), 14.

[58] John Doble, Jared Bosk, and Samantha DuPont, *Public Thinking about Coping with the Cost of Health Care: How Do We Pay for What We Need? Outcomes of the 2008 National Issues Forums* (Dayton, OH: A Public Agenda Report for the Kettering Foundation, June 2009), 4–5. This report is based on research involving more than 1,000 citizens in deliberative forums held in 40 states and the District of Columbia.

[59] David Holwerk, "A Public Voice: A Long-Running Experiment Bears Promising Fruit," *Connections* (2013): 22–23.

[60] For more information on this experiment, contact the National Coalition for Dialogue & Deliberation (www.ncdd.org).

[61] See Brendan Greeley, "Making Sense of the Games Politicians Play," *Bloomberg Businessweek*, August 30, 2012, http://www.businessweek.com/articles/2012-08-30/making-sense-of-the-games-politicians-play (accessed October 8, 2012).

[62] "Public goods" has been defined as the things people build or organize to benefit everyone: they can include everything from playgrounds for children to neighborhood watches, to environmental protection coalitions.

[63] Monica Schoch-Spana et al., "Community Engagement: Leadership Tool for Catastrophic Health Events," *Biosecurity and Bioterrorism: Biodefense Strategy, Practice, and Science* 5, no. 1 (2007): 8–25. Also see Rebecca Solnit, *A Paradise Built in Hell: The Extraordinary Communities that Arise in Disaster* (New York: Viking Press, 2009).

[64] Public Agenda, *Still the Best in the World? An Exploratory Study of Americans' Views on the Legal System Today* (Dayton, OH: Draft report to the Kettering Foundation, April 2012).

[65] The three issue guides, *". . . And Justice for All": Ensuring Public Trust and Confidence in the Justice System* (2001), *Reaching a Verdict: What Do We Want for the American Jury System?* (2005), and *Under Pressure: How Can We Keep the Courts Fair and Impartial?* (2007), were prepared by the American Bar Association in collaboration with the National Issues Forums Institute and the Kettering Foundation.

[66] Albert W. Dzur, *Punishment, Participatory Democracy, and the Jury* (New York: Oxford University Press, 2012).

[67] Robert D. Putnam, Robert Leonardi, and Raffaella Y. Nanetti, *Making Democracy Work: Civic Traditions in Modern Italy* (Princeton, NJ: Princeton University Press, 1993) and Vaughn L. Grisham Jr., *Tupelo: The Evolution of a Community* (Dayton, OH: Kettering Foundation Press, 1999).

[68] Doble Research Associates, *How People Connect: The Public and Public Schools* (Dayton, OH: Report to the Kettering Foundation, June 1998), 5.

[69] Among the seemingly invincible forces that deny people the ability to shape their future, none is cited more often than those of the global corporate

world. This is not the place to analyze this perception, but I would note that there is a literature on the constructive role business can play in civic life, such as Daniel Yankelovich's *Profit with Honor: The New Stage of Market Capitalism* (New Haven, CT: Yale University Press, 2006).

13. Reflections

[1] See the empirical data on the importance of collective efficacy reported by Robert J. Sampson in *Great American City: Chicago and the Enduring Neighborhood Effect* (Chicago: University of Chicago Press, 2012), 368.

[2] Nick McNamara, "Social and Public Deliberation Reflection" (class assignment in Dr. Wanda Minor's course titled Social and Public Deliberation, Monmouth University, West Long Branch, NJ, April 2011).

[3] This idea was introduced in Edward N. Lorenz, "Predictability: Does the Flap of a Butterfly's Wings in Brazil Set off a Tornado in Texas?" (paper presented to the American Association for the Advancement of Science, Washington, DC: December 29, 1972).

BIBLIOGRAPHY

Alter, Theodore R. "Achieving the Promise of Public Scholarship." In *Engaging Campus and Community: The Practice of Public Scholarship in the State and Land-Grant University System*, edited by Scott J. Peters, Nicholas R. Jordan, Margaret Adamek, and Theodore R. Alter, 461–487. Dayton, OH: Kettering Foundation Press, 2005.

Annenberg Institute on Public Engagement for Public Education. *Reasons for Hope, Voices for Change.* Providence, RI: Annenberg Institute for School Reform, 1998.

Arendt, Hannah. *Between Past and Future: Eight Exercises in Political Thought.* New York: Penguin Books, 1977.

Arens, Sheila A. *Examining the Meaning of Accountability: Reframing the Construct, a Report on the Perceptions of Accountability.* Aurora, CO: Mid-continent Research for Education and Learning (McREL), July 2005.

Aristotle. *The Ethics of Aristotle: The Nicomachean Ethics.* Translated by J. A. K. Thomson. London: Penguin Books, 1953.

Barber, Benjamin. *Strong Democracy: Participatory Politics for a New Age.* Berkeley: University of California Press, 1984.

Barker, Derek W. M. "The Colonization of Civil Society." *Kettering Review* 28, no. 1 (Fall 2010): 8–18.

————. "From Associations to Organizations: Tocqueville, NGOs, and the Colonization of Civic Leadership." In *Alexis de Tocqueville and the Art of Democratic Statesmanship*, edited by Brian Danoff and L. Joseph Hebert Jr., 205–223. Lanham, MD: Lexington Books, 2011.

Barker, Derek W. M., Noëlle McAfee, and David W. McIvor, eds. *Democratizing Deliberation: A Political Theory Anthology*. Dayton, OH: Kettering Foundation Press, 2012.

Batie, Sandra S. "Wicked Problems and Applied Economics." *American Journal of Agricultural Economics* 90, no. 5 (2008): 1176–1191.

Berry, Wendell. *The Unsettling of America: Culture and Agriculture*. San Francisco: Sierra Club Books, 1986.

Bilby, Sheila Beachum. "Community School Reform: Parents Making a Difference in Education." *Mott Mosaic* 1 (December 2002): 3.

Bishop, Bill, with Robert G. Cushing. *The Big Sort: Why the Clustering of Like-Minded America Is Tearing Us Apart*. New York: Houghton Mifflin, 2008.

Bockmeyer, Janice L. "A Culture of Distrust: The Impact of Local Political Culture on Participation in the Detroit EZ." *Urban Studies* 37, no. 13 (December 2000): 2417–2440.

Boyd, T. A. *Professional Amateur: The Biography of Charles F. Kettering*. New York: E.P. Dutton, 1957.

Boyte, Harry C. *The Backyard Revolution: Understanding the New Citizen Movement*. Philadelphia: Temple University Press, 1980.

————. "The Growth of Citizen Politics: Stages in Local Community Organizing." *Dissent* 37 (Fall 1990): 516.

Boyte, Harry C., and Nancy N. Kari. *Building America: The Democratic Promise of Public Work*. Philadelphia: Temple University Press, 1996.

Brady, Marion. "Thinking Big: A Conceptual Framework for the Study of Everything." *Phi Delta Kappan* (December 2004): 276–281.

Brecher, Jeremy. "'If All the People Are Banded Together': The Naugatuck Valley Project," *Labor Research Review* 1, no. 9, article 10 (1986): 1–17.

Brecher, Jeremy, and Tim Costello, eds. *Building Bridges: The Emerging Grassroots Coalition of Labor and Community*. New York: Monthly Review Press, 1990.

Briggs, Xavier de Souza. *Democracy as Problem Solving: Civic Capacity in Communities across the Globe*. Cambridge, MA: MIT Press, 2008.

Brown, David W. *When Strangers Cooperate: Using Social Conventions to Govern Ourselves*. New York: The Free Press, 1995.

Bruhn, John G., and Stewart Wolf. *The Roseto Story: An Anatomy of Health*. Norman: University of Oklahoma Press, 1979.

Cahn, Edgar S. *No More Throw-Away People: The Co-Production Imperative*, 2nd ed. Washington, DC: Essential Books, 2004.

Campbell, Cole C. "Journalism and Public Knowledge." *Kettering Review* (Winter 2007): 39–49.

Carcasson, Martín. *Democracy's Hubs: College and University Centers as Platforms for Deliberative Practice*. Dayton, OH: Kettering Foundation, 2008.

Christman, Jolley Bruce, and Amy Rhodes. *Civic Engagement and Urban School Improvement: Hard-to-Learn Lessons from Philadelphia*. Philadelphia, PA: Consortium for Policy Research in Education, 2002.

Comer, James P. *Waiting for a Miracle: Why Schools Can't Solve Our Problems—And How We Can*. New York: Dutton, 1997.

Cook, Brian J. *Bureaucracy and Self-Government: Reconsidering the Role of Public Administration in American Politics*. Baltimore, MD: The Johns Hopkins University Press, 1996.

———. *Democracy and Administration: Woodrow Wilson's Ideas and the Challenges of Public Management*. Baltimore, MD: The Johns Hopkins University Press, 2007.

Cremin, Lawrence A. *American Education: The Colonial Experience, 1607-1783*. New York: Harper and Row, 1970.

———. *American Education: The Metropolitan Experience, 1876-1980*. New York: Harper and Row, 1988.

————. *American Education: The National Experience, 1783-1876.* New York: Harper and Row, 1980.

Crenson, Matthew A., and Benjamin Ginsberg. *Downsizing Democracy: How America Sidelined Its Citizens and Privatized Its Public.* Baltimore, MD: The Johns Hopkins University Press, 2002.

Crim, Alonzo A. "A Community of Believers Creates a Community of Achievers." *Educational Record* 68/69 (fall 1987/winter 1988): 45.

Crockett, Connie. "Communities as Educators: A Report on the November 2007 Public and Public Education Workshop." *Connections* (2008): 22–24.

Damasio, Antonio. *Descartes' Error: Emotion, Reason, and the Human Brain.* New York: Penguin Books, 2005.

De Martino, Benedetto, Dharshan Kumaran, Ben Seymour, and Raymond J. Dolan. "Frames, Biases, and Rational Decision-Making in the Human Brain." *Science* 313, no. 5787 (August 4, 2006): 684–687.

Dennison, George M. *The Dorr War: Republicanism on Trial, 1831-1861.* Lexington: University Press of Kentucky, 1976.

Derthick, Martha. "Crossing Thresholds: Federalism in the 1960s." In *Keeping the Compound Republic: Essays on American Federalism.* Washington, DC: Brookings Institution Press, 2001.

————. *The Influence of Federal Grants: Public Assistance in Massachusetts.* Cambridge, MA: Harvard University Press, 1970.

Dewey, John. *The Public and Its Problems: An Essay in Political Inquiry,* edited by Melvin L. Rogers. University Park: Pennsylvania State University Press, 2012.

Dittmer, John. *Local People: The Struggle for Civil Rights in Mississippi.* Urbana: University of Illinois Press, 1994.

Dubnick, Melvin, and H. George Frederickson. *Accountable Governance: Problems and Promises.* New York: M.E. Sharpe, 2011.

Dye, Thomas R., Harmon Zeigler, and Louis Schubert. *The Irony of Democracy: An Uncommon Introduction to American Politics,* 15th ed. Boston: Wadsworth, Cengage Learning, 2012.

Dzur, Albert W. "Four Theses on Participatory Democracy: Toward the Rational Disorganization of Government Institutions." *Constellations* 19, no. 2 (2012): 305–324.

———. *Punishment, Participatory Democracy, and the Jury*. New York: Oxford University Press, 2012.

Elazar, Daniel J., and John Kincaid. "Covenant and Polity." *New Conversations* 4, no. 2 (Fall 1979): 4–8.

Ellerman, David. "Good Intentions: The Dilemma of Outside-In Help for Inside-Out Change." *The Nonprofit Quarterly* (Fall 2006): 46–49.

Evans-Pritchard, E. E. *The Nuer: A Description of the Modes of Livelihood and Political Institutions of a Nilotic People*. New York: Oxford University Press, 1969.

Fagotto, Elena, and Archon Fung. *Sustaining Public Engagement: Embedded Deliberation in Local Communities*. East Hartford, CT: An Occasional Research Paper from Everyday Democracy and the Kettering Foundation, 2009.

Fauconnier, Gilles, and Mark Turner. *The Way We Think: Conceptual Blending and the Mind's Hidden Complexities*. New York: Basic Books, 2002.

Fear, Frank A., Cheryl L. Rosaen, Richard J. Bawden, and Pennie G. Foster-Fishman. *Coming to Critical Engagement: An Autoethnographic Exploration*. Lanham, MD: University Press of America, 2006.

Follett, Mary Parker. *The New State: Group Organization the Solution of Popular Government*. New York: Longmans, Green and Company, 1920.

Ford, Pat. *Don't Stop There! Five Adventures in Civic Journalism*, edited by Jan Schaffer. Washington, DC: The Pew Center for Civic Journalism, 1998.

Frederickson, H. George. *Easy Innovation and the Iron Cage: Best Practice, Benchmarking, Ranking, and the Management of Organizational Creativity*. Dayton, OH: Kettering Foundation, June 2003.

Gaillard, Frye, Sheila Hagler, and Peggy Denniston. *In the Path of the Storms: Bayou La Batre, Coden, and the Alabama Coast*. Auburn, AL: Pebble Hill Books, Auburn University and Tuscaloosa, AL: The University of Alabama Press, 2008.

Gaventa, John, and Gregory Barrett. *So What Difference Does It Make? Mapping the Outcomes of Citizen Engagement*, IDS Working Paper, 347. Brighton, UK: Institute of Development Studies, 2010.

Gillmor, Dan. *We the Media: Grassroots Journalism by the People, for the People*. Sebastopol, CA: O'Reilly Media, 2004.

Gordon, Edmund W., and Michael A. Rebell. "Toward a Comprehensive System of Education for All Children." *Teachers College Record* 109, no. 7 (2007): 1836–1843.

Grisham, Vaughn L., Jr. *Tupelo: The Evolution of a Community*. Dayton, OH: Kettering Foundation Press, 1999.

Gunderson, Lance H., and C. S. Holling, eds. *Panarchy: Understanding Transformations in Human and Natural Systems*. Washington, DC: Island Press, 2002.

Gutmann, Amy, and Dennis Thompson. *Why Deliberative Democracy?* Princeton, NJ: Princeton University Press, 2004.

Habermas, Jürgen. "Three Normative Models of Democracy." *Constellations: An International Journal of Critical and Democratic Theory* (April 1994): 1–10.

Hanson, Sandra L., and John Kenneth White. "The Making and Persistence of the American Dream." In *The American Dream in the 21st Century*, edited by Sandra L. Hanson and John Kenneth White, 1–16. Philadelphia: Temple University Press, 2011.

Harbour, Patricia Moore. *Community Educators: A Resource for Educating and Developing Our Youth*. Dayton, OH: Kettering Foundation Press, 2012.

Harding, Heather. "Supplementary Education: Educating and Developing the Whole Child, An Interview with Edmund W. Gordon." In *Understanding Educational Equity and Excellence at Scale*. Providence, RI: The Annenberg Institute for School Reform at Brown University, 2007.

Harriger, Katy J., and Jill J. McMillan. "Public Scholarship and Faculty Role Conflict." *Higher Education Exchange* (2005): 17–23.

———. *Speaking of Politics: Preparing College Students for Democratic Citizenship through Deliberative Dialogue.* Dayton, OH: Kettering Foundation Press, 2007.

Harwood, Richard C. *Citizens and Politics: A View from Main Street America.* Dayton, OH: Kettering Foundation, 1991.

———. *Hope Unraveled: The People's Retreat and Our Way Back.* Dayton, OH: Kettering Foundation Press, 2005.

———. *The Work of Hope: How Individuals and Organizations Can Authentically Do Good.* Dayton, OH: Kettering Foundation Press, 2012.

Harwood, Richard C., and John A. Creighton. *The Organization-First Approach: How Programs Crowd Out Community.* Bethesda, MD: Kettering Foundation and The Harwood Institute for Public Innovation, 2009.

The Harwood Group. *Meaningful Chaos: How People Form Relationships with Public Concerns.* Dayton, OH: Kettering Foundation, 1993.

———. *Forming Public Capital: Observations from Two Communities.* Dayton, OH: Report to the Kettering Foundation, August 1995.

———. *Strategies for Civil Investing: Foundations and Community-Building.* Dayton, OH: Report to the Kettering Foundation, 1997.

———. *Squaring Realities: Governing Boards and Community-Building.* Dayton, OH: Kettering Foundation, 2000.

The Harwood Institute for Public Innovation. *The Engagement Path: The Realities of How People Engage over Time—and the Possibilities for Re-engaging Americans.* Washington, DC: Harwood Institute, 2003.

Henderson, Anne T., and Karen L. Mapp. *A New Wave of Evidence: The Impact of School, Family, and Community Connections on Student Achievement.* Austin, TX: Southwest Educational Development Laboratory, 2002.

Hibbing, John, and Elizabeth Theiss-Morse. *Stealth Democracy: Americans' Beliefs about How Government Should Work*. New York: Cambridge University Press, 2002.

Holwerk, David. "A Public Voice: A Long-Running Experiment Bears Promising Fruit." *Connections* (2013): 22–23.

Isocrates. "Antidosis." In *Isocrates*, vol. 2. Translated by George Norlin. 1929. Reprint, New York: G.P. Putnam's Sons, 2000.

Johnson, Jean, Jonathan Rochkind, and Samantha DuPont. *Don't Count Us Out: How an Overreliance on Accountability Could Undermine the Public's Confidence in Schools, Business, Government, and More*. New York and Dayton, OH: Public Agenda and Kettering Foundation, 2011.

Kari, Nan, and Nan Skelton. *Voices of Hope: The Story of the Jane Addams School for Democracy*. Dayton, OH: Kettering Foundation Press, 2007.

Kettering Foundation. *Speaking of Public Journalism: Talks from the Project on Public Life and the Press—Seminars at the American Press Institute, 1993–1997*. Dayton, OH: Kettering Foundation, 1997.

———. *Too Many Children Left Behind: How Can We Close the Achievement Gap?* Dayton, OH: Kettering Foundation, 2007.

———. *Helping Students Succeed: Communities Confront the Achievement Gap*. Dayton, OH: Kettering Foundation, 2010.

———. *Naming and Framing Difficult Issues to Make Sound Decisions: A Kettering Foundation Report*. Dayton, OH: Kettering Foundation, 2011.

Kiesa, Abby, Alexander P. Orlowski, Peter Levine, Deborah Both, Emily Hoban Kirby, Mark Hugo Lopez, and Karlo Barrios Marcelo. *Millennials Talk Politics: A Study of College Student Political Engagement*. College Park, MD: CIRCLE, The Center for Information & Research on Civic Learning & Engagement, 2007.

Kingdon, John W. *Agendas, Alternatives and Public Policies*, 2nd ed. New York: Addison-Wesley Educational Publishers, 2003.

Kretzmann, John P., and John L. McKnight. *Building Communities from the Inside Out: A Path toward Finding and Mobilizing a Community's Assets*. Chicago: ACTA Publications, 1993.

———. *Voluntary Associations in Low-Income Neighborhoods: An Unexplored Community Resource, A Case Study of Chicago's Grand Boulevard Neighborhood*. Evanston, IL: The Asset-Based Community Development Institute, Institute for Policy Research, Northwestern University, 1996.

Leighninger, Matt. *The Next Form of Democracy: How Expert Rule Is Giving Way to Shared Governance . . . and Why Politics Will Never Be the Same*. Nashville, TN: Vanderbilt University Press, 2006.

———. "Is Everything Up to Date in Kansas City? Why 'Citizen Involvement' May Soon Be Obsolete." *National Civic Review* (Summer 2007): 12–27.

Levine, Peter. "Learning and Democracy: Civic Education." *Kettering Review* (Fall 2006): 32–42.

———. *We Are the Ones We Have Been Waiting For: The Promise of Civic Renewal in America*. New York: Oxford University Press, 2013.

Lippmann, Walter. *The Phantom Public*. 1927. Reprint, New Brunswick, NJ: Transaction Publishers, 2004.

London, Scott. *Investing in Public Life: A Report from the 2003-2004 Dialogues on Civil Investing*. Dayton, OH: Kettering Foundation and Pew Partnership for Civic Change, 2005.

———. *Doing Democracy: How a Network of Grassroots Organizations Is Strengthening Community, Building Capacity, and Shaping a New Kind of Civic Education*. Dayton, OH: Kettering Foundation, 2010.

———. *Informal Networks: The Power of Organic Community Groups*. Dayton, OH: A Harwood Institute Report Prepared for the Kettering Foundation, 2010.

Mansbridge, Jane. *Beyond Adversary Democracy*. Chicago: University of Chicago Press, 1983.

———. "Everyday Talk in the Deliberative System." In *Deliberative Politics: Essays on Democracy and Disagreement.* Edited by Stephen Macedo. Oxford: Oxford University Press, 1999.

Mathews, David. "Creating a Movement toward 'Civil Philanthropy.'" *The Chronicle of Philanthropy* 7 (April 20, 1995): 42–43.

———. *For Communities to Work.* Dayton, OH: Kettering Foundation, 2002.

———. *Is There a Public for Public Schools?* Dayton, OH: Kettering Foundation Press, 1996.

———. *Politics for People: Finding a Responsible Public Voice*, 2nd ed. Chicago: University of Illinois Press, 1999.

———. *Reclaiming Public Education by Reclaiming Our Democracy.* Dayton, OH: Kettering Foundation Press, 2006.

———. *Why Public Schools? Whose Public Schools? What Early Communities Have to Tell Us.* Montgomery, AL: NewSouth Books, 2003.

McKnight, John. *The Four-Legged Stool.* Dayton, OH: Kettering Foundation, 2013.

McNath, Robert C., Jr. *American Populism: A Social History, 1877-1898.* New York: Hill and Wang, 1993.

Meier, Christian. *The Greek Discovery of Politics.* Translated by David McLintock. Cambridge, MA: Harvard University Press, 1990.

Milstein, Bobby. *Hygeia's Constellation: Navigating Health Futures in a Dynamic and Democratic World.* Atlanta, GA: Centers for Disease Control and Prevention, 2008.

Molnar-Main, Stacie, with Libby Kingseed. "Public Learning in Public Schools: How Networks of Teachers and Public Partners Can Support Civic Learning." *Connections* (2013): 28–30.

Morse, Suzanne W. *Smart Communities: How Citizens and Local Leaders Can Use Strategic Thinking to Build a Brighter Future.* San Francisco: Jossey-Bass, 2004.

Mulenburg, Jerry. "Crew Resource Management Improves Decision Making." *Ask Magazine: The NASA Source for Project Management and Engineering Excellence* 42 (Spring 2011): 11–13.

Neblo, Michael A., Kevin M. Esterling, Ryan P. Kennedy, David M. J. Lazer, and Anand E. Sokhey. "Who Wants to Deliberate—And Why?" *American Political Science Review* 104, no. 3 (August 2010): 566–583.

Nelson, William E. *The Roots of American Bureaucracy, 1830-1900.* Cambridge, MA: Harvard University Press, 1982.

Nielsen, Randall. "Public Schools and the Practices of Engaged Communities." *Connections* (April 2004): 20.

Oldenburg, Ray. *The Great Good Place: Cafés, Coffee Shops, Bookstores, Bars, Hair Salons, and Other Hangouts at the Heart of a Community.* New York: Marlowe, 1999.

Ostrom, Elinor. *Governing the Commons: The Evolution of Institutions for Collective Action.* Cambridge: Cambridge University Press, 1990.

———. "Covenanting, Co-Producing, and the Good Society." *The Newsletter of PEGS (Committee on the Political Economy of the Good Society)* 3, no. 2 (Summer 1993): 7–9.

———. "Beyond Markets and States: Polycentric Governance of Complex Economic Systems." *American Economic Review* 100, no. 3 (June 2010): 641–672.

Page, Benjamin I., and Robert Y. Shapiro. *The Rational Public: Fifty Years of Trends in Americans' Policy Preferences.* Chicago: University of Chicago Press, 1992.

Pennekamp, Peter H., and Anne Focke. *Philanthropy and the Regeneration of Community Democracy.* Dayton, OH: Kettering Foundation, 2013.

Perkin, Harold. *The Rise of Professional Society: England since 1880.* New York: Routledge, 1990.

Peters, Scott J., with Theodore R. Alter and Neil Schwartzbach. *Democracy and Higher Education: Traditions and Stories of Civic Engagement.* East Lansing, MI: Michigan State University Press, 2010.

Pilisuk, Marc, and Susan Hillier Parks. *The Healing Web: Social Networks and Human Survival.* Hanover, NH: University Press of New England, 1986.

Piven, Frances Fox, and Richard Cloward. *Poor People's Movements: Why They Succeed, How They Fail.* New York: Vintage Books, 1979.

Postel, Charles. *The Populist Vision.* New York: Oxford University Press, 2007.

Public Agenda and Kettering Foundation. *Will It Be on the Test? A Closer Look at How Leaders and Parents Think about Accountability in the Public Schools.* New York and Dayton: Public Agenda and Kettering Foundation, 2013.

Putnam, Robert D. *Bowling Alone: The Collapse and Revival of American Community.* New York: Simon & Schuster, 2000.

————. "Community-Based Social Capital and Educational Performance." In *Making Good Citizens: Education and Civil Society,* edited by Diane Ravitch and Joseph P. Viteritti. New Haven, CT: Yale University Press, 2001.

Putnam, Robert D., and Lewis M. Feldstein. *Better Together: Restoring the American Community.* New York: Simon & Schuster, 2003.

Putnam, Robert D., Robert Leonardi, and Raffaella Y. Nanetti. *Making Democracy Work: Civic Traditions in Modern Italy.* Princeton, NJ: Princeton University Press, 1993.

Rahn, Wendy M., and Thomas Rudolph. "A Tale of Political Trust in American Cities." *Public Opinion Quarterly* 69, no. 4 (2005): 530–560.

Rittel, Horst W. J., and Melvin M. Webber. "Dilemmas in a General Theory of Planning." *Policy Sciences* 4 (1973): 155–169.

Rokeach, Milton, and Sandra J. Ball-Rokeach. "Stability and Change in American Value Priorities, 1968–1981." *American Psychologist* 44 (May 1989): 775–784.

Rosen, Jay. *What Are Journalists For?* New Haven, CT: Yale University Press, 1999.

Ross, Carne. *The Leaderless Revolution: How Ordinary People Will Take Power and Change Politics in the Twenty-first Century.* New York: Blue Rider Press, 2011.

Safford, Sean. *Why the Garden Club Couldn't Save Youngstown: The Transformation of the Rust Belt*. Cambridge, MA: Harvard University Press, 2009.

Sampson, Robert J. *Great American City: Chicago and the Enduring Neighborhood Effect*. Chicago: University of Chicago Press, 2012.

Sanz de Santamaría, Alejandro. "Education for Political Life." *Kettering Review* (Winter 1993), 9–18.

Sartori, Giovanni. *The Theory of Democracy Revisited*. Chatham, NJ: Chatham House Publishers, 1987.

Schoch-Spana, Monica, Crystal Franco, Jennifer B. Nuzzo, and Christiana Usenza. "Community Engagement: Leadership Tool for Catastrophic Health Events." *Biosecurity and Bioterrorism: Biodefense Strategy, Practice and Science 5*, no. 1 (2007): 8–25.

Scott, James C. *Seeing Like a State: How Certain Schemes to Improve the Human Condition Have Failed*. New Haven, CT: Yale University Press, 1998.

Seymour, Ben, and Ray Dolan. "Emotion, Decision Making, and the Amygdala." *Neuron* 58 (June 12, 2008): 662–668.

Shelton, Jack. *Consequential Learning: A Public Approach to Better Schools*. Montgomery, AL: NewSouth Books, 2005.

Sievers, Bruce. "Can Philanthropy Solve the Problems of Civil Society?" *Kettering Review* (December 1977): 62–70.

———. *Civil Society, Philanthropy, and the Fate of the Commons*. Medford, MA: Tufts University Press, 2010.

Sirianni, Carmen, and Lewis Friedland. *Civic Innovation in America: Community Empowerment, Public Policy, and the Movement for Civic Renewal*. Berkeley: University of California Press, 2001.

Skocpol, Theda. *Protecting Soldiers and Mothers: The Political Origins of Social Policy in the United States*. Cambridge, MA: Belknap Press of Harvard University Press, 1992.

———. "The Narrowing of Civic Life." *The American Prospect* 15 (June 2004): A5–7.

———. "Reinventing American Civic Democracy." *Kettering Review* 28 (Fall 2010): 49–60.

Solnit, Rebecca. *A Paradise Built in Hell: The Extraordinary Communities That Arise in Disaster*. New York: Viking Press, 2009.

Stone, Clarence N. "Linking Civic Capacity and Human Capital Formation." In *Strategies for School Equity: Creating Productive Schools in a Just Society*, edited by Marilyn J. Gittell. New Haven, CT: Yale University Press, 1998.

Tocqueville, Alexis de. *Democracy in America*. Translated by Harvey C. Mansfield and Delba Winthrop. Chicago: University of Chicago Press, 2000.

Warren, Mark E. "When, Where and Why Do We Need Deliberation, Voting, and Other Means of Organizing Democracy? A Problem-Based Approach to Democratic Systems." Paper prepared for delivery at the American Political Science Association annual meeting, New Orleans, LA, August 30–September 2, 2012.

Warren, Mark R. *Dry Bones Rattling: Community Building to Revitalize American Democracy*. Princeton, NJ: Princeton University Press, 2001.

Weber, Max. *Economy and Society*. Edited by Guenther Roth and Claus Wittich. Berkeley: University of California Press, 1978.

Welter, Rush. *Popular Education and Democratic Thought in America*. New York: Columbia University Press, 1962.

Wharton, Tony, ed. *Journalism as a Democratic Art: Selected Essays by Cole C. Campbell*. Dayton, OH: Kettering Foundation Press, 2012.

Wiebe, Robert H. *The Search for Order, 1877-1920*. New York: Hill and Wang, 1967.

———. *Self-Rule: A Cultural History of American Democracy*. Chicago: University of Chicago Press, 1995.

Wilson, Mark, and Nan Fairley. "Living Democracy: A Project for Students and Citizens." *Higher Education Exchange* (2012): 35–47.

Wilson, Woodrow. *The New Freedom: A Call for the Emancipation of the Generous Energies of a People*. New York: Doubleday, Page and Company, 1913.

————. "The Study of Administration." In *Classics of Public Administration*, 2nd ed., edited by Jay M. Shafritz and Albert C. Hyde. Chicago: The Dorsey Press, 1987.

Woodruff, Paul. *First Democracy: The Challenge of an Ancient Idea.* New York: Oxford University Press, 2005.

Yankelovich, Daniel. *Coming to Public Judgment: Making Democracy Work in a Complex World.* Syracuse, NY: Syracuse University Press, 1991.

————. *Profit with Honor: The New Stage of Market Capitalism.* New Haven, CT: Yale University Press, 2006.

Yankelovich, Daniel, and Will Friedman, eds. *Toward Wiser Public Judgment.* Nashville, TN: Vanderbilt University Press, 2010.

Zakaria, Fareed. *The Post-American World, Release 2.0.* New York: W. W. Norton, 2008.

INDEX